Juno's

NATURE EMBROIDERY NOTEBOOK

Stitching Plants, Animals, and Stories

ユノ
JUNO

SCHIFFER CRAFT
4880 Lower Valley Road • Atglen, PA 19310

Preface

Embroidery floss makes my heart dance.

The threads shine like glittering jewels and there are just so many colors.

It's fun simply to line up the threads and think thoughts like these: "The changing colors of the summer sky, shifting from evening to night" or "The color change of a fresh young rose as it gradually loses its moisture and that lovely red color that deepens until the petals fall in a flurry."

A variety of stitches are used to transform these beautiful threads into something magnificent. Even the most complicated stitches aren't that scary if you follow the steps one by one. And even the simplest stitches begin to possess overwhelming magic if you line many of them up side by side.

This book is a collection of examples that show how I have used the power of thread and stitching to give shape to my ideas. The most important thing is to stitch with a joyful heart. Please transform my notebook into your own notebook and reference; don't necessarily follow the instructions given. Let your imagination flow freely and move your hands with intent—this will allow you to work wonders with your mind.

I hope this book gives you a guide to help release, and give shape to, your inner creativity.

Juno

Contents

Cavansite
Amazonite
Spinel
Boltwoodite
DesertRose

Botanical Motif Embroidery

Carefully observe a plant and trace its characteristics one stitch at a time—be sure to include the strength and evanescence of that plant.

This particular piece of flower embroidery was freely stitched to appear as if a lot of flowers were just scattered about. The shapes, directions, and sizes of the flowers are all different. Stitching in a natural and free way is more difficult than stitching with a certain pattern of course, but try it out and just do what your heart desires. Feel free to adopt and change the pattern on p. 82 as you wish.

Embroidery Pattern: see p. 82

Dried mimosa flowers can be enjoyed for a long time after their blooms are past their prime. Their glowing yellow color changes to a more subdued shade as they age. Looking closely at the small and firm flowers, you will see that they look like a cluster of grains. They remind me of knots. It should be noted that embroidery floss is a perfect medium to express the mimosa's feathery foliage.. The flowers can be worked using a French knot stitch, but I purposefully used a plain knot stitch in such a way as to show smooth and round sides.

Embroidery Pattern: see p. 66

An example of the mimosa design on p. 8. Beautiful flowing branches of mimosa surround the neck of the gown. Try embroidering this on a favorite blouse!

The image of freshly picked chamomile—scattered about as if its scent is flowing through the air—was chosen for the embroidery on this round-bottomed drawstring pouch. Make the yellow center three-dimensional to produce a delightful look and to give it a pleasant touch. Try stitching some side-facing or rear-facing flowers as well, not just the front-facing ones.

Instructions: see p. 68

As if overflowing a pocket, this design expresses excitement to me. Embroider this design on the chest pocket of either a plain shirt or a blouse. If the pocket is already attached and it is difficult to embroider the design as is, attempt to carefully remove the pocket, embroider, and then reattach the pocket. If you want to make your own pocket, cotton or linen plain weave fabric is most suitable. The flowers themselves are stitched using a turkey rug stitch that loops with each stitch.

Embroidery Pattern: see p. 70

The dandelion has a round flower and its fluff lightly flies away. It also has deep, deep roots that penetrate the earth. I stitched this design to show not only the sprightliness of the dandelion, but also to show its vitality by aligning the roots with the spine. Feel free to change the length of the roots depending on your chosen material.

Embroidery Pattern: see p. 72

Thriving under gentle sunlight, these springtime flowers have a gentle appearance. I stitched them as if I were gently rubbing the soft, plump leaves; the gracefully curved stems; and the petals full of faintly changing colors. I used a single strand of embroidery floss to work the petals and other intricate layers of color so that they don't become too thick. After stitching on thick sheeting fabric, make a bag and attach a sturdy flat strap. The end result is simple and rustic. It's as if a drawing in a sketchbook is embellishing the bag.

Instructions: see p. 74

I chose my favorite designs from the dried flowers on p. 20 and then combined them to make these purses. The metal clasps are antique gold that matches the color of the dried flowers. I like to make purses with metal clasps because of their shape and practicality.

Instructions: see p. 78

I find withering flowers and their dull colors to be quite beautiful. Actually, I find both the freshness of springtime flowers—as expressed on p. 16—and the dull and subdued appearance of dried flowers to be equally stunning. They are just in different states. I should also mention here that I prefer to design things in a random manner rather than making a perfect layout.

Embroidery Pattern: see p. 80

When making small items from scratch, I take great pleasure in incorporating something that will make the user happy. When you open these envelope-shaped butterfly cases, it looks as if butterflies are flying over flowers. The top case is colorful and realistic, while the bottom is simple and uses subdued colors. Feel free to use fabric that has your preferred texture and color and also to alter the case size as needed.

Instructions: see p. 83

Small details, such as the eyes and the lay of the fur, can affect any animal's expression. That is why animal motifs are fun, but also difficult to embroider. Perhaps that is as it should be, however, given that we are attempting to capture various aspects of living things with embroidery.

Using single animal motif embroidery on a ready-made simple shirt. Fluffy and fuzzy animals—embroidered with relaxed expressions—create a strong contrast with the plain shirt. The unexpected cuteness will surely warm the hearts of any who see it.

Embroidery Pattern: see p. 86

For each design, work the bushy parts with turkey rug stitch. Cut and trim off the loops of the stitch to produce a fluffy look.

Top left: The hedgehog's belly is a tiny little pocket! The spines and facial parts are first stitched separately and then put together later.
Bottom right: Work the fox's bushy tail last. Carefully change colors of floss, starting with the tip of the tail.
Top right, Bottom left: After cutting the turkey rug stitch loops, carefully trim off the floss, using the tip of your scissors. This will produce a three-dimensional effect for both the polar bear and the donkey. Even if the floss is the same color, the trimmed area will look darker.

Use turkey rug stitching to create fluffy cat fur. It is difficult to control stitch detail with this method, but at the very least it will have a humorous effect.

It looks like there are a bunch of cats having a meeting on this cushion. If you have a fun idea, don't worry about practicality; just give it a shot. It's not easy to embroider such large surfaces, so remember that embroidering even a single cat is plenty to create a cute item. Do you have a cat? Feel free to choose your favorite colors based off your own pets!

Instructions: see p. 89

Use turkey rug stitch to create the plump cat paws. The face of the cat is not stitched, but if you were to look inside the pocket, you could imagine seeing the face of your favorite cat. Pay attention to the positioning of the paws, in relation to the pocket, since they will be ruined if the pocket hangs down too much!

Instructions: see p. 92

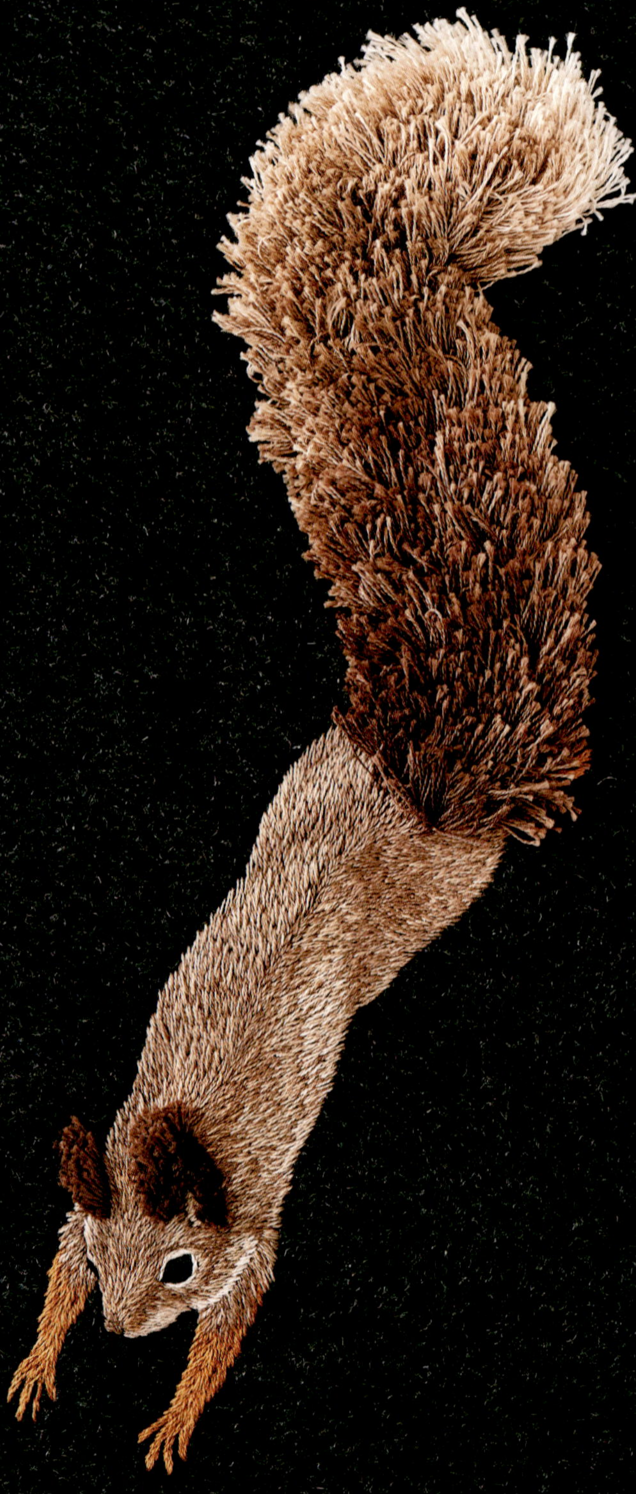

A little buddy who goes everywhere with you. When I used to watch cartoons as a child, I longed for just such a pal. Even though I'm an adult now, no one would be offended if I embroidered a cheerful little squirrel on my blanket and wrapped myself up in it at my house, all smiles and warmth.

Instructions: see p. 94

Swallows fly in and build their nests under the eaves of people's houses in the spring. The swallow's tail is split in two, kind of like human legs. That makes them somewhat familiar looking. The clear shape of the wings makes them easy to create, and the stitching is so pleasant that I want to make them again and again.

Embroidery Pattern: see p. 96

Wings make an attractive motif. Not only do I admire them for their ability to produce flight, but I also think they are genuinely beautiful in shape and structure. Even though the direction of flow is uniform, each strand is stitched a little randomly to create a three-dimensional effect. After filling in the center with the flow of feather, and keeping it in mind, adjust the outline with long and short stitches by wrapping the edge. This allows you to achieve a beautiful finished look.

Embroidery Pattern: see p. 97

Swallows in various forms of flight. I originally thought that swallows must like to fly and have fun, but it turns out that they aren't playing. They are actually preying on insects! Still, eating while flying seems like it would be fun. In a way, this bag design captures the essence of swallows at mealtime.

Embroidery Pattern: see p. 98

"Shapes Found in Nature" Motif Embroidery

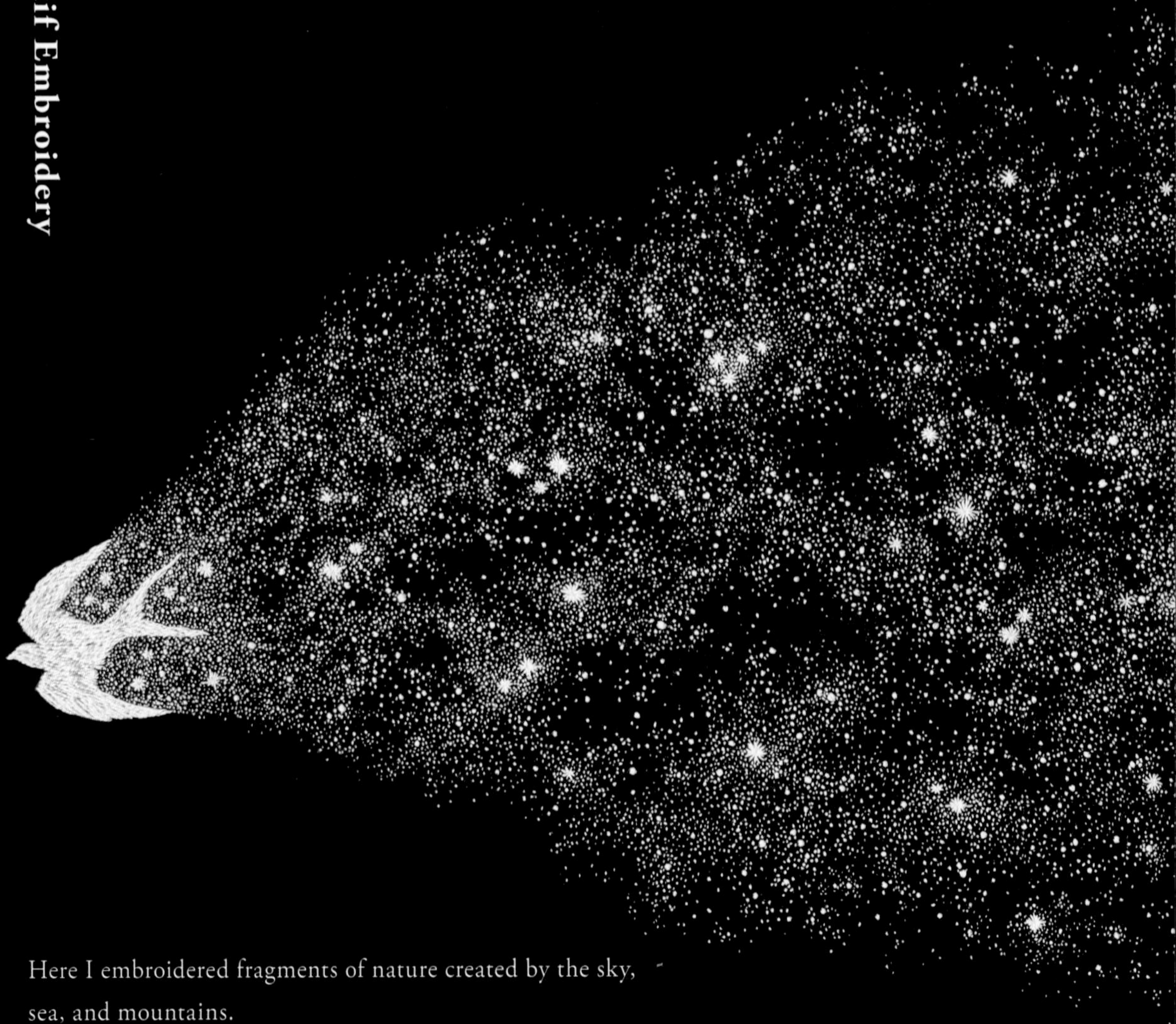

Here I embroidered fragments of nature created by the sky, sea, and mountains.
When you look at them, again and again you will see many strange and interesting shapes.

"Galaxy Swallow" flies at high speed through space. Its body is made of light particles, so it looks like shooting stars from the ground . . . One of the joys of handcrafts is the freedom to express scenes from any story that comes to mind. This design uses one color of embroidery floss and simple stitches and just keeps stitching endlessly without any particular layout. Be careful; if you stitch nonchalantly, you may lose track of time and become too immersed in your work. Actually, it's hard to immerse yourself in a project when you're trying to stitch exactly as you envision or when you're concerned with efficiency. Sometimes, when you focus on the act of stitching, you can go beyond your imagination and become immersed in a sense of security that exists only in the present moment. It's more like meditation than anything else.

Embroidery Pattern: see p. 106

"Galaxy Swallow" is made with a simple but powerful stitch. Here, the design is placed across the hem of a black dress we might find in a witch's closet. Depending on the light, the drape of the fabric appears to change colors—appearing like galaxies or the Northern Lights—which stimulates our imagination of the universe. This design can be worked spontaneously. Find your favorite item to embroider and it might be fun to expand the galaxy by adding stitches from time to time, while still using the item on a daily basis.

Lustrous embroidery floss is good for creating sharp textures. Crystals can be fibrous or fluffy, and surprisingly, embroidery floss can effectively express the texture of gemstones. Embroider the name of the gemstones in a coaching stitch—you will feel like a collector!

Embroidery Pattern: see p. 100

It is said that crystals have a lot of power. This bookmark is like a talisman, combining your favorite crystal with its meaning and your favorite words. Every time I open a book, I feel a little reassured.

Instructions: see p. 102

It is said that everything on earth is made of the same material. I wonder if this is why things from the sea and things from the mountains have similar shapes. When I lined them up neatly and framed them, they looked like a specimen box. I think the interesting shapes stand out more when you stitch them without using a lot of colors.

Instructions: see p. 103

Books and Embroidery

My life consists mainly of embroidery and reading, and books have influenced me a lot. But I think the two books by Michael Ende that I read as a child have been the most important for my embroidery. My unceasing desire to "blend fantasy into everyday life" is nurtured by *The Neverending Story*. In addition, my belief is that—as was taught by *Momo*—"One should spend time unstintingly, saving time brings about a spiritless mind."

Embroidery is a very time-consuming process, but if you think of it as a way to "savor the moment," the urgency to complete the work and the impatience with slow progress will disappear. In the end, you will be able to get more done with this attitude. When I work silently with my hands, people sometimes say that it looks like some kind of meditation. I don't mind meditation, but lately I like to think of myself as a wizard. I am a wizard who connects their inner world with reality.

Rather than getting ideas for designs directly from books, I often learn more about my mind or my attitude. For example, from books like *Zen* by D. T. Suzuki and *Otona no onna ga utsukusii (Mature Women Are Beautiful)* by Setsu Nagasawa. As a book on embroidery, *Shishu no ABC (The ABCs of Embroidery)* by Ayako Otsuka is a book that I have always cherished. It is full of ideas and a sense of style that doesn't feel old even today. I am filled with joy to know that such simple embroidery can make an ordinary day seem special.

I always feel like I am being told to "be yourself and express yourself" by books that give me guidance. They are like beacons of light at the end of a dark tunnel. Sometimes my thoughts try to interrupt my progress, but I force myself to keep stitching, and I absorb myself in the creative aspect of my work. I feel like my work is a part of myself and brings me joy.

Travel and Embroidery

There have been two occasions when I have suddenly become curious about a certain ethnic group. As I gathered more and more information, I just let it flow and started my trip. On these two occasions, I visited the Shipibo people, living in the Peruvian Amazon, and the Leng Teng people, living deep in the mountains of Laos.

Both groups were of Asian descent, with faces and builds that were familiar to me as a Japanese person. Many of the women worked all day doing embroidery, dyeing, and other fabric-related handiwork. The two groups also have something in common in the way they work on handicrafts leisurely while chatting outside or relaxing in a hammock during the day. Also, in the way they stitch beautifully without using embroidery hoops. It was very reassuring to know that it is possible to continue to create such joyful and beautiful things with only a minimum of tools. In addition, I felt that what I was doing (embroidering) must be a very instinctive act.

The current situation, in 2020, doesn't allow us to travel easily. However, if the opportunity presents itself again—like it did in the past—I would like to travel and again go with the flow and let things happen.

Leng Teng Tribe Embroidery

The Leng Teng people spin yarn from cotton, weave fabric, dye it with plant dyes, embroider it, and then make things with it—all by hand! Their spontaneous and humorous embroidery expresses to me their freedom and the love of their daily lives.

Shipibo Tribe Embroidery

The Shipibo people, who live in the Peruvian rainforest, believe in the power of shamanism. Their unique geometric patterns represent life energy vibrations. They use the power of plants—such as ayahuasca and piri-piri—to turn their visions into embroidery and mud-dye patterns.

Myanmar Naga Tribe Embroidery

I came across Naga embroidery at a specialty store in Onomichi, Okayama prefecture. I thought the puzzled, face-like pattern was cute. However, I later found out that Nagas history includes headhunting. That made me think that this motif might be. . . well, I don't really know what to think.

Memories of Embroidery

I stitched freely, recalling memories and scenery as if I were just doodling in a diary or rough sketching.

The lacelike stitches express the translucency of thin lemon slices. Organza is a little difficult to work with, but it brings out the sheer look of lemon. This work encapsulates my memory of a sweet and sour summer.

This is a simple bag made by sewing the side seams of organza that has been folded in half. The seams are wrapped with ribbon. The bag is see-through, so anything inside is visible. You can put dried flowers inside and make a nice little home décor item. You can also use it as a wonderful piece of gift packaging for a small item.

Instructions: see p. 107

I thought these coarse linen summer pants looked like a sandy beach. So, I embroidered people enjoying their vacation at the beach on them. By pairing with a light-blue shirt, you can create the idea of a summer beach scene. On this work, the embroidery was applied from the hips to the waist, but feel free to adapt the pattern and embroider as desired.

Embroidery Pattern: see p. 108

The impressive snow-covered mountains may look overwhelming to stitch. However, the embroidered area is not that large, since this work actually makes use of the natural shirt color. For stitching the people enjoying skiing, make use of leftover embroidery floss and stitch freely. Use any color you want. Similar to the beach scenery embroidered pants, you can embroider this design on anything. But, if you are embroidering on a ready-made shirt, try to incorporate the buttons into the design.

Embroidery Pattern: **see p. 110**

Footprints of Embroidery Floss

When embroidering, I try to avoid wasting thread.

Patterns on the reverse side of the embroidery actually possess a nuanced feel that cannot be created intentionally.

It is as if an impressionist painter lives in my subconscious, and that is why I love to look at the reverse side.

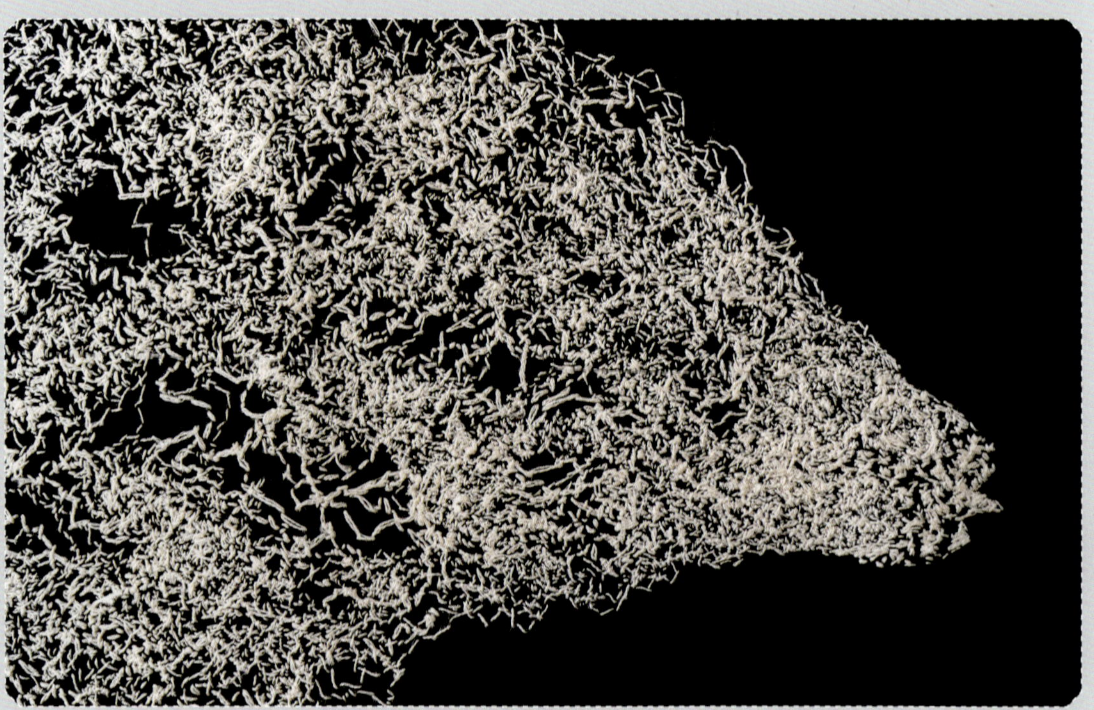

The backside of "Galaxy Swallow" is quite chaotic.
On the front side, the stitches are dots, but on the backside, the dots are connected by lines even though they are close to each other. The result sort of looks like a bunch of interesting footprints.

Embroidery showing the backside of my dried flowers design. On the backside, they actually look more fragile.

Skiing embroidery.
I feel that the ambiguous shapes and popping threads here on the backside give it more of a sense of speed.

Tools

Let me introduce tools I use. Choose your own preferred hoops and embroidery needles.

1. Hoop: 10 cm / 4" hoop. Wrap a ribbon around the frame when embroidering thin fabric. **2. Scissors:** You need both embroidery scissors and fabric shears. Use sharp embroidery scissors with a pointed tip. **3. Embroidery Needles and Pincushion:** Size 8 and 9 French embroidery needles. Choose depending on the number of strands. **4. Marking Pencil or Pen:** For transferring patterns onto fabric or marking fabric for cutting/sewing. Use water-erasable marking pens. After stitching is complete, be sure to soak your project in water to erase any lines. **5. Tracing Paper:** Used to transfer patterns without making photocopies. **6. Ruler:** A bamboo ruler. **7–9. Stylus, Cellophane (OPP plastic bag), Chalk-Based Transfer Paper:** Used to transfer patterns onto fabric.

Materials

Choose your desired embroidery floss and fabric. You can enjoy colors while you embroider.

1. Various Types of Fabric: Along with linen and cotton, this book also uses wool and organza. **2. Ribbon:** Organza ribbon is used to make bookmarks. **3. DMC No. 25 six-stranded Embroidery Floss:** In various colors. Since this book uses three different colors to stitch one petal, it is best to have them in gradations.

Stitching Instructions

Here are the stitches used in this book, and my own stitching method.

❋ Pattern Transfer

1 Place transfer paper and pattern on fabric then secure with pins. Lay cellophane on top and trace the pattern with a stylus.

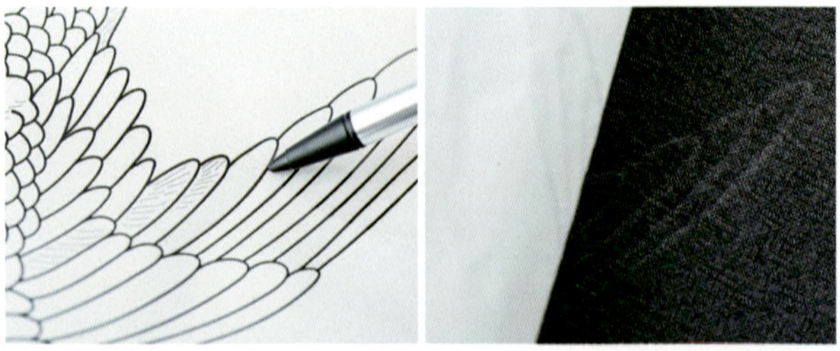

2 Over the cellophane, trace pattern firmly, using a stylus to mark fabric.

❋ Start of Stitch

Start with backstitch.

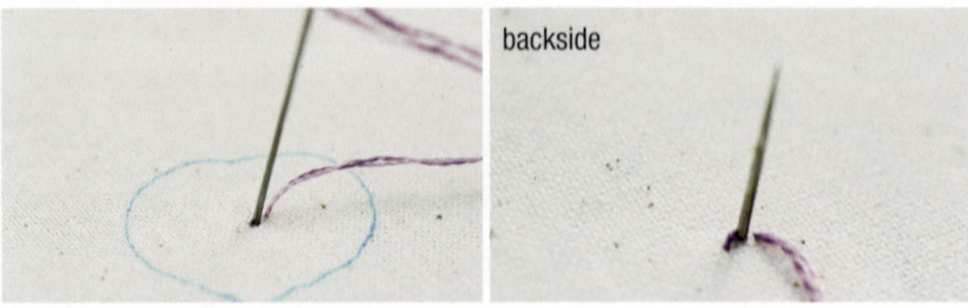

Bring the needle up through the fabric. Make a small stitch, then backstitch to fasten the laid floss.

Start with knot

Tie a knot at end of the floss and start stitching. As an example, the mimosa flower in this book begins this way.

❋ Disposing of Floss

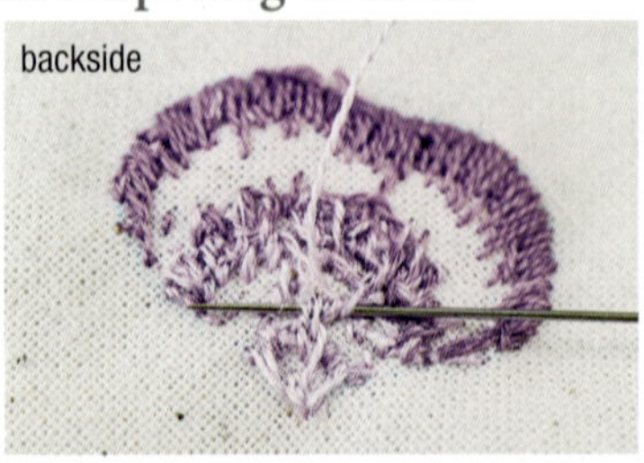

On the backside, slide needle under floss twice and then cut.

❋ Outline Stitch

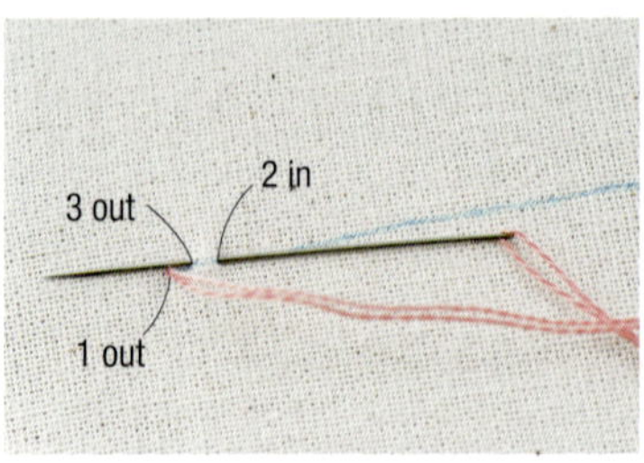

1 Stitch from left to right along pattern lines. Make one stitch and bring the needle up through the fabric at a point halfway along the length of the previous stitch.

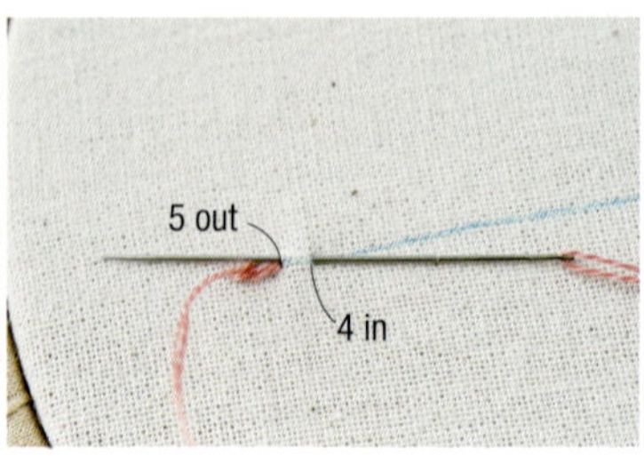

2 Repeat by bringing the needle up at a point halfway along the length of the previous stitch.

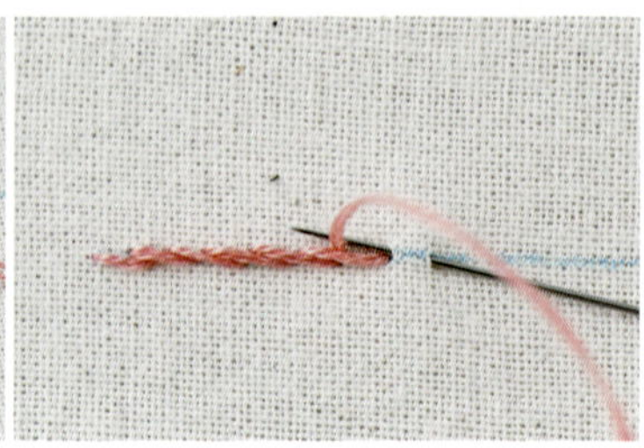

3 Make sure stitch lengths are uniform in order to produce beautiful stitches.

⁂ Couching Stitch

1 Uses two pieces of floss. The left floss lays on the pattern and the right fastens down the laid-down piece.

2 Lay floss on surface along the pattern line. Fasten with the other floss.

3 Fasten the laid-down floss at regular intervals.

⁂ Satin Stitch

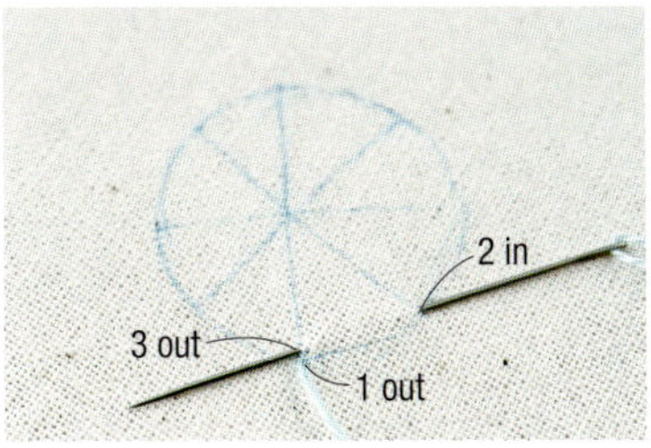

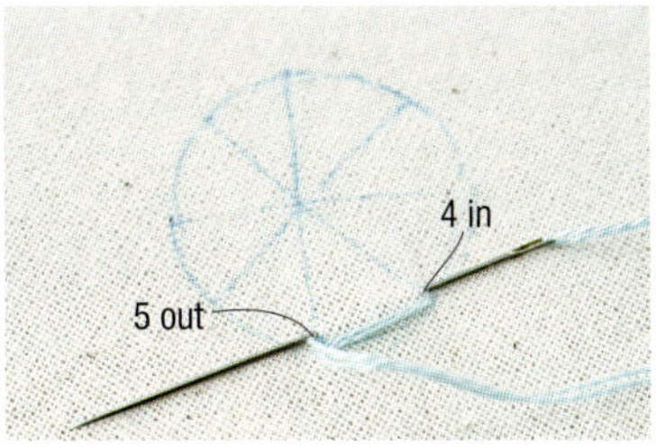

1 Used to fill entire areas of a pattern. Pull needle out, then push it back in at desired length. Bring it up again next to where the initial stitch exited.

2 Make second stitch parallel to first stitch.

3 Repeat steps noted above to fill area.

⁂ Chain Stitch

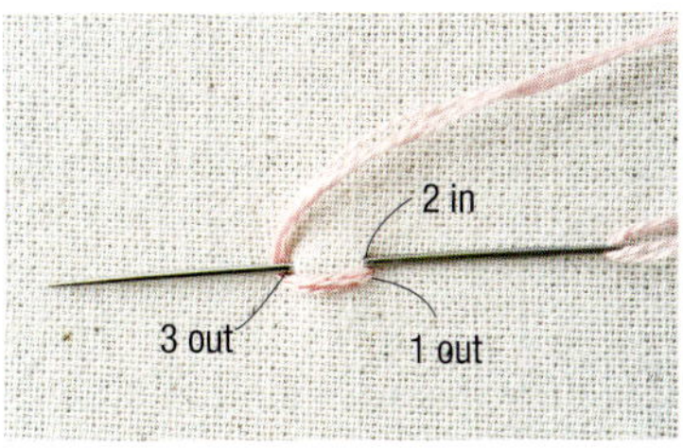

1 Bring needle up. Insert needle next to initial exit point. Next, bring needle back up at desired stitch length. Loop floss around needle tip and pull needle out (do not overtighten).

2 Next, insert the needle down through the fabric right next to where the needle came up on the previous stitch. Bring the needle up a stitch length away and loop the floss around the needle.

3 Repeat the steps to produce a chain. Push needle down through the fabric at the bottom of the last loop to finish.

⁂ Lazy Daisy Stitch

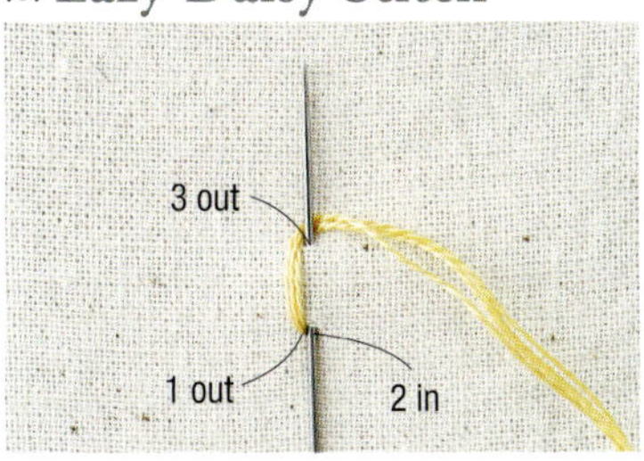

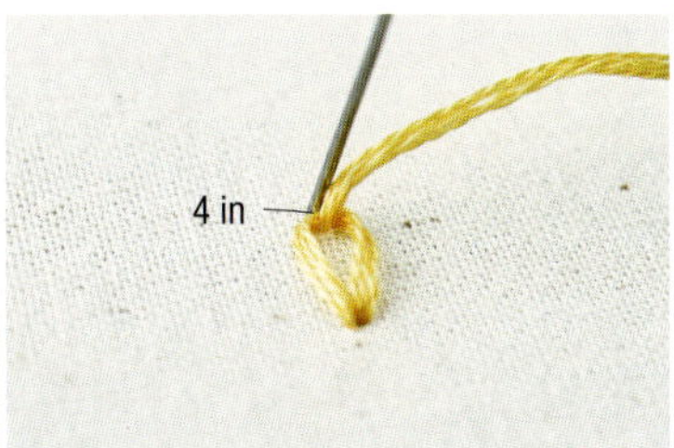

1 The lazy daisy stitch is similar to the chain stitch except that each link is worked individually. Bring needle up, then insert a very short distance from the initial exit point. Push needle through at desired stitch length, loop floss around needle tip, and pull.

2 Push needle back in above the edge of the loop.

3 Repeat the steps above as desired. Working the stitch in a circular shape makes a flower.

❋ Bullion Stitch

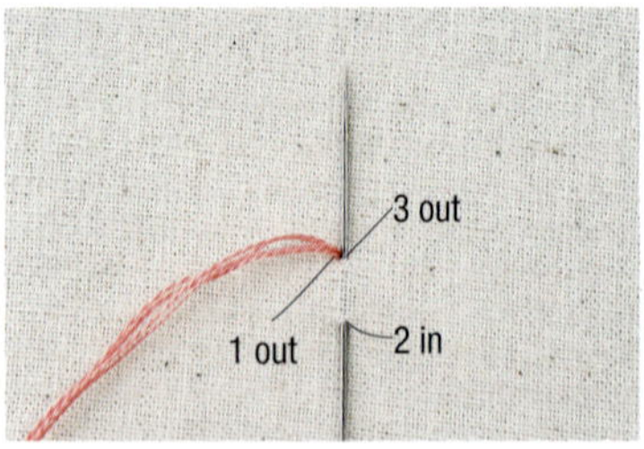

1 Bring needle up through fabric. Then, push it back through at desired stitch length. Bring needle back up right next to the initial exit point.

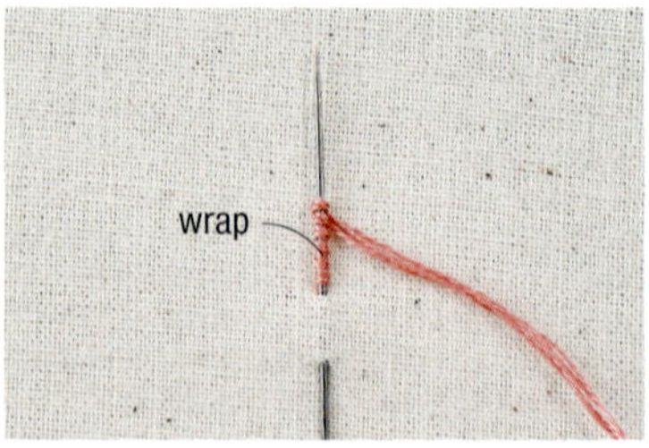

2 Don't pull needle through yet. Wrap floss around needle several times. Make sure the wraps are a little longer than the stitch length.

3 Hold spiral with thumb to prevent it from loosening. Pull needle through.

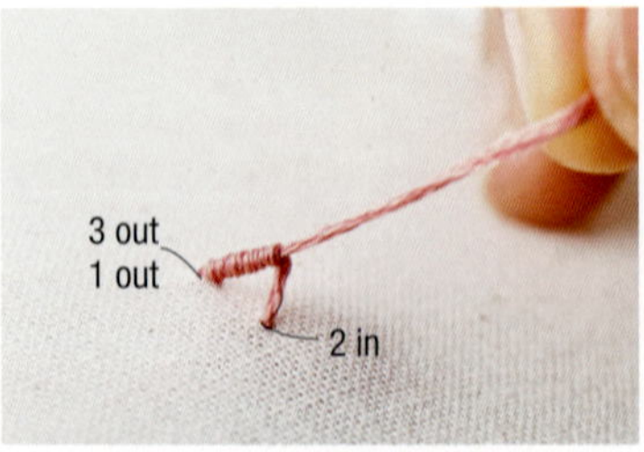

4 Pull floss upward to keep spiral in place.

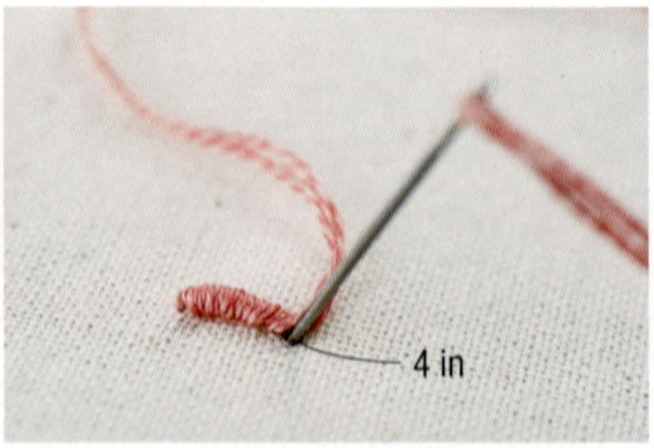

5 Insert needle right next to the point where it went into the fabric in step 1.

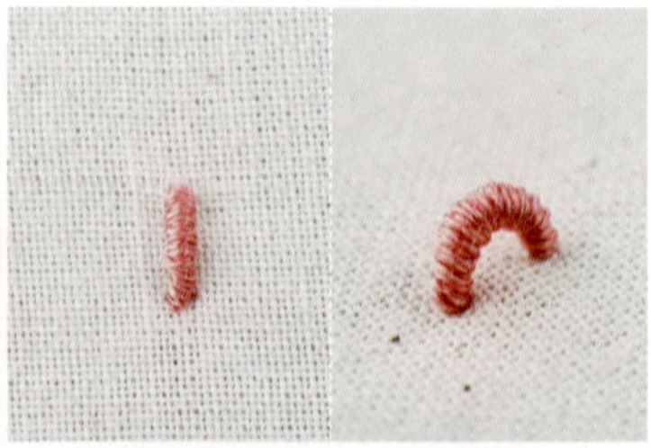

6 Your bullion stitch is complete. If the spiral is longer than the stitch, the knot curves in an arch, as seen in the photo.

❋ Lace Filling Stitch

1 Embroider the rind and membrane walls first. Bring the needle up from the backside of the membrane wall. Scoop a stitch on the rind.

2 Without pulling the floss all the way through, loop it around the needle and lightly pull through. Repeat by scooping a stitch on the rind a short distance away.

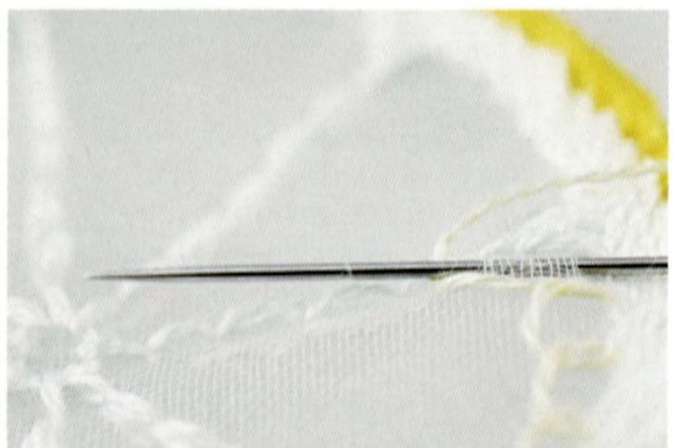

3 Once you have stitched all the way to the adjacent membrane wall, bring needle through fabric at membrane wall edge and lay working floss under needle, same as blanket stitch. Pull needle through.

4 Insert needle through membrane wall and move on to next segment. Do this along each membrane wall to secure floss.

5 Repeat steps and work along rind. The first row is complete. Bring needle through membrane wall a little inside the first row and proceed to work on second row. Bring needle out through backside of first row.

6 Repeat while bringing needle through first-row loops to stitch all around. Don't forget to secure with blanket stitch at each membrane wall and other important positions. The loops should be different sizes to produce a natural look.

⁂ Stumpwork Buttonhole Stitch

1 Create an outline stitch for the length of the pattern.

2 Push needle to backside. Slide floss under and wrap each stitch on backside of fabric. Continue until beginning of first stitch.

3 Bring needle up through fabric, slightly above the outline stitch. Slide the needle under one outline stitch. Before pulling floss all the way through, put needle through the loop, from right to left.

4 Repeat, sliding the needle under each outline stitch and pushing it through the loop of working floss.

5 Once you reach the end on right, slide the needle under each loop from top to bottom and go back to left end.

6 Once at left end, insert needle through both the leftmost outline stitch and the fabric.

7 Repeat steps 3 and 4. For step 3, slide the needle under each outline stitch, but this time slide it under each loop created in step 4.

8 Once at right edge, push needle both through the loop and the fabric. Go back to left edge while sliding needle under each loop as in step 5.

9 Repeat the steps above for the required number of rows to complete buttonhole.

⁂ Blanket Stitch

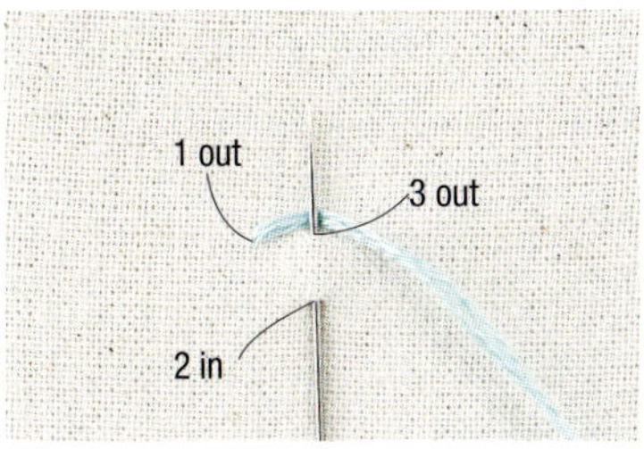

1 Bring needle up through fabric and then insert perpendicularly through fabric. Lay floss under the needle and pull it through.

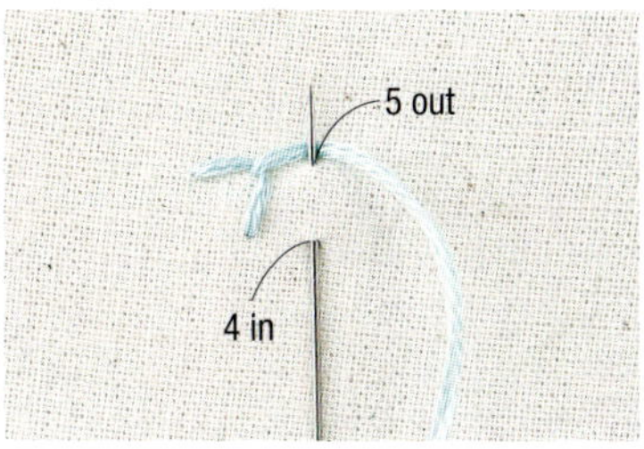

2 Insert needle perpendicularly and bring it up through the fabric at regular intervals. Lay floss under the needle and pull it through.

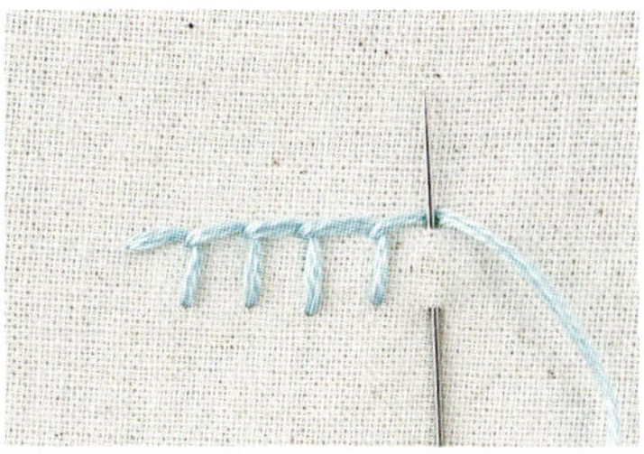

3 Repeat steps until you reach desired length.

⁂ Random Stitching

This method is similar to the satin stitch and long & short stitch, but slightly different. Stitches are uniform in direction but worked randomly to vary their length and width. This method enables you to express the texture of animal fur and to produce a three-dimensional effect.

Stitching Mimosa

⁂ Backstitch

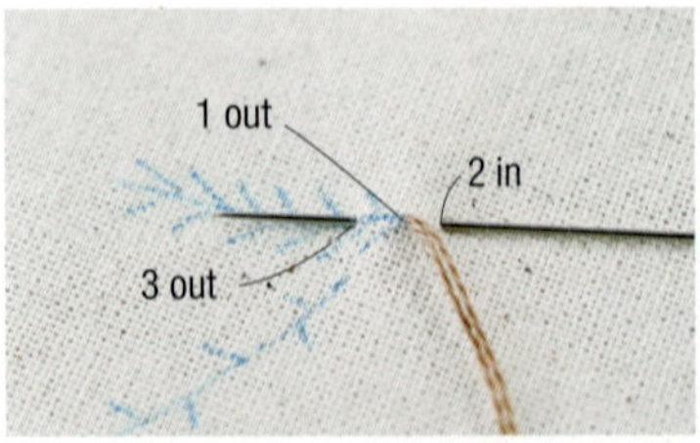

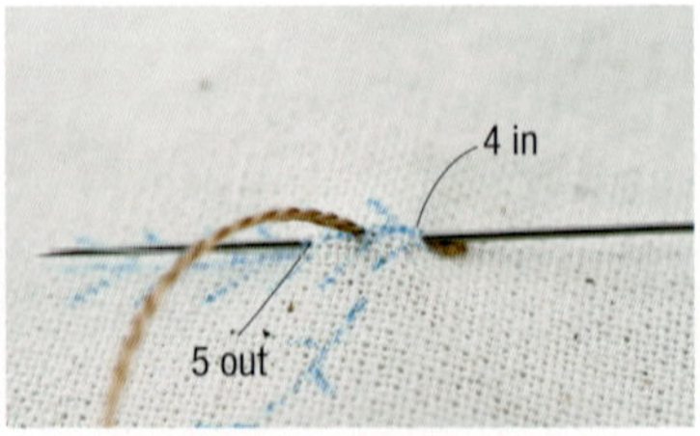

1 Bring needle up through fabric on marked line. Go back about half the stitch length back from where needle came out, then insert needle. Bring it up again half the stitch length ahead of where it initially came out.

2 In the same way, insert the needle at the end of the previous stitch and then bring it up at the desired distance from the previous stitch.

3 Repeat these steps. Work from right to left.

⁂ Straight Stitch

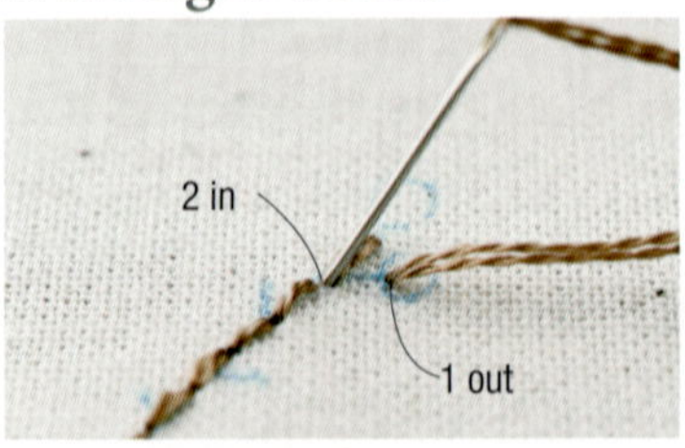

1 After back-stitching mimosa's main branch, start to make stems by straight stitching. Bring needle up through fabric onto marked line and stitch according to marked lines.

2 Work stems in a zigzag pattern. Bring needle up on opposite side of the branch and stitch in the same manner.

3 Use four strands of embroidery floss and straight stitch for the leaves. Since four strands of embroidery floss are used, the same straight stitch as the stems will produce thicker lines here.

⁂ Knot Flower

1 Bring needle up through fabric and lay it down where the needle came out. Wrap floss around needle tip once. Push floss down with your thumb and pull needle all the way through. You now have a knot.

2 Push needle down next to knot and pull all the way through fabric.

3 This completes the knot flower. This method produces a side-facing knot that turns the round and lustrous side of the knot up. Make knots in a cluster to produce the raised lumps that look just like a flower.

Stitching a Petal

✻ Long & Short Stitch

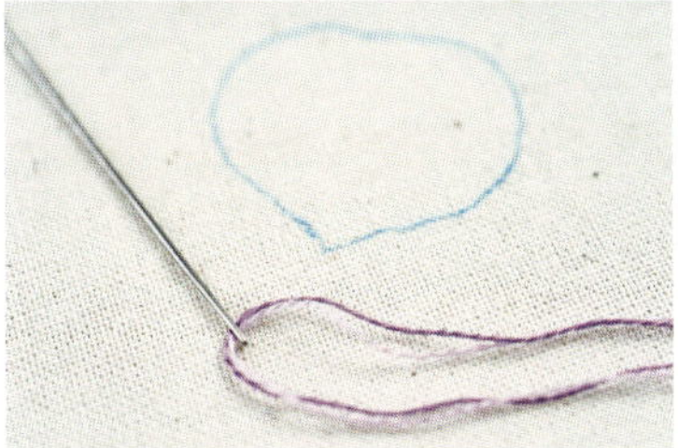

1 Transfer pattern onto fabric. Use two strands of embroidery floss. Both should be similar in color, one a darker shade and the other lighter.

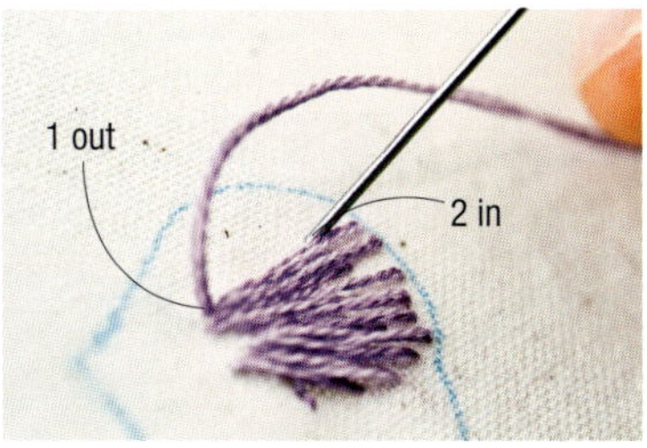

2 Begin stitching at center of pattern. Make stitches of desired length.

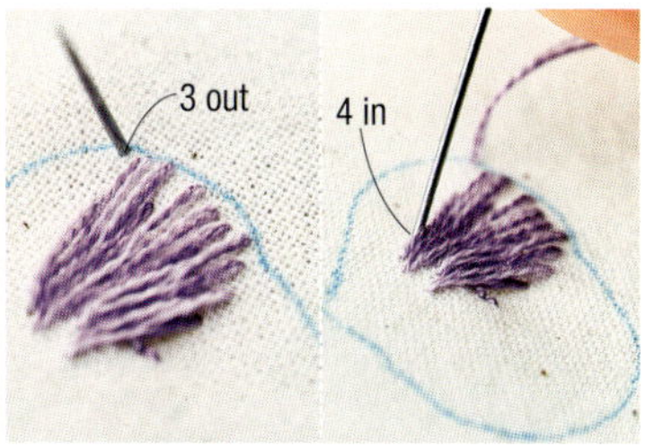

3 Bring needle up through fabric next to previous stitch. Make stitches of desired length. Since they are made side by side, close together, the floss travels less on the backside.

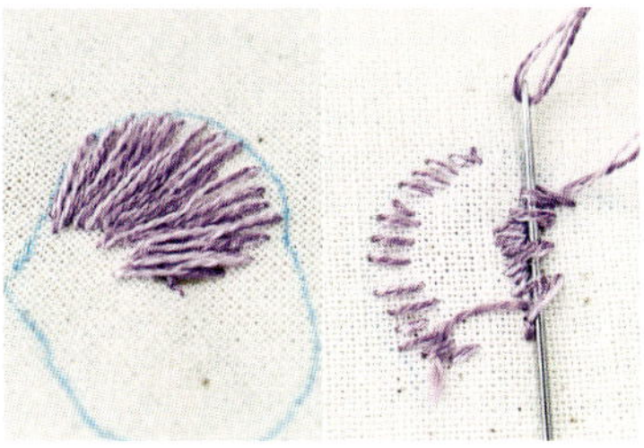

4 Once you have reached the pattern edge, return to center, where you started. Slide needle under laid floss on backside to return to center.

5 Bring needle up through fabric next to first stitch at center. Then, fill other half in the same manner.

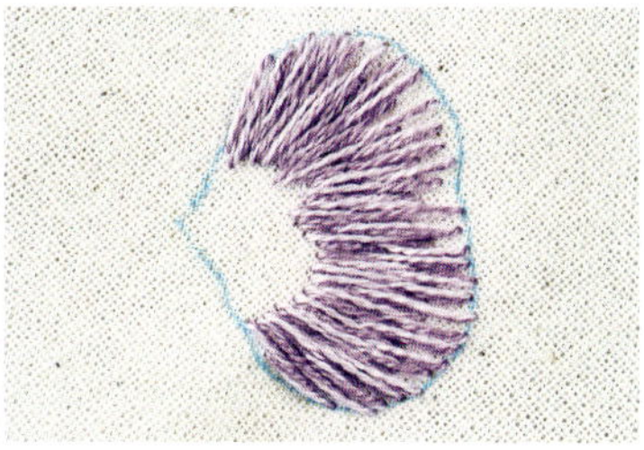

6 First row is complete.

7 Next, fill pattern edge and shape petal. Use single strand of floss. Start from edge.

8 Fill area along edge according to pattern. Here, instead of bringing needle up right next to previous stitch, go in from edge and bring needle up at a random stitch length.

9 Once edge is full, fill in extra places to blend border between first row and edge. Use a single strand of floss.

10 Next, work on petal base. Use two strands of same-colored floss and stitch in the same way as the first row. The second row is complete. It's okay if the border between the first and second rows isn't completely filled at this point.

11 Use single-strand floss and fill in spaces to blend the border between the first and second rows.

12 Fill remaining area at petal base, using single-strand floss. The petal is now complete. The petal has depth and volume due to the use of three different-colored pieces of floss. They are different shades of the same color.

Turkey Rug Stitch Flower

❋ Turkey Rug Stitch

1 Bring needle up through fabric. Make a 0.1 cm / 1/16" long stitch, then bring needle back up at a point 0.1 cm / 1/16" away from previous stitch.

2 In the same manner as step 1, make a 0.1 cm / 1/16" long stitch and bring needle up 0.1 cm / 1/16" away from previous stitch. Pull floss, but leave a 1 cm / 3/8" wide loop with remaining working floss.

3 Push needle down through fabric 0.2 cm / 1/16" behind current stitch and then bring it up next to end of loop. This completes one turkey rug stitch.

4 Push needle down through fabric 0.2 cm / 1/16" away from floss tail and make a loop without pulling floss all the way through. Bring needle up 0.1 cm / 1/16" away from loop end and pull floss all the way. Push needle down through fabric 0.2 cm / 1/16" behind current stitch and up right next to last loop end, creating something similar to a backstitch.

5 Repeat process and work along pattern all the way around. This is a repetition of a forward stitch to make a loop and a backstitch to secure the base of the loop.

6 Stitch using same technique for second row. The flower petals are complete, if you choose to have looped petals.

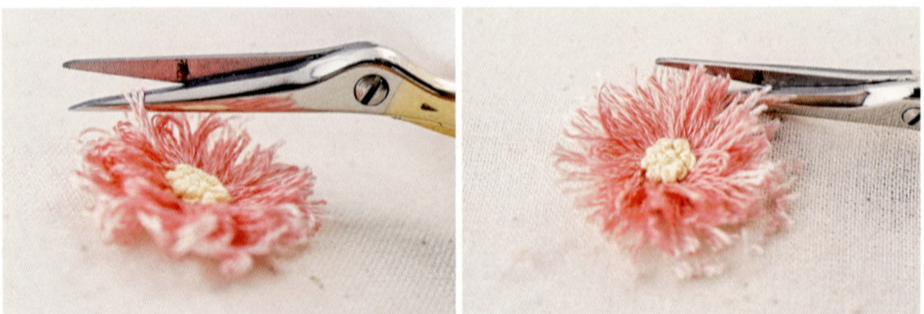

7 The method for adjusting the shape by cutting loops: First cut the loops and then trim them to the desired length to produce the intended effect.

Turkey Rug Stitch

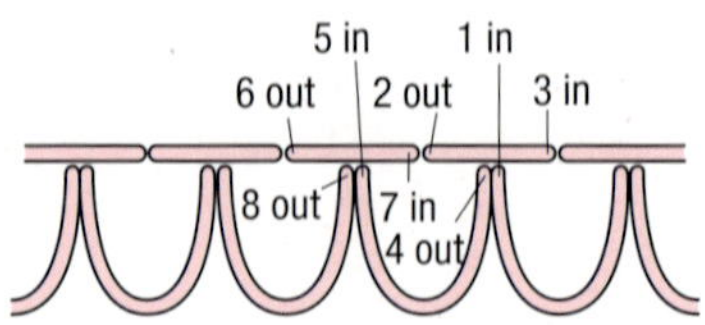

❋ French Knot Stitch

1 Push floss up through fabric. Lay needle down and wrap floss once around tip.

2 Push needle back down at a point very close to where it came out. Pull the needle through perpendicular to backside.

3 This makes a small ball. Make several French knots for the flower center and hide base of turkey rug stitches.

Patterns and Instructions

- The unit of measurement used here is primarily, and most precisely, cm. Though this book also provides measurements in inches, remember that they are approximate conversions only.
- Figure dimensions and patterns do not include seam allowances unless otherwise indicated. Add 1 cm / ⅜" seam allowance. Cut fabric without adding a seam allowance where labeled "No seam allowance."
- Fabric sizes given have some room for adjustments.
- Prepare fabric that is thick enough to be stable in an embroidery hoop.
- The letter "S" in diagrams is an abbreviation for stitch. The abbreviation RS stands for right side, and WS stands for wrong side of fabric.
- Completed work dimensions may differ from measurements given on diagrams.
- This book lists DMC embroidery floss color numbers. But feel free to use your preferred materials. Enjoy combining your favorite embroidery flosses and colors.
- Patterns without enlargement scales are full-sized. Where enlargement scales are specified, make enlarged copies accordingly.

p. 8 Mimosa

80% Scale Pattern. Enlarge the 80% scale pattern to 125% to produce full-size pattern.

⁜ Embroidering Instructions

1. Backstitch the branches.
2. Use straight stitch for the leaves. Where necessary, stitch by combining four single-color strands and a four-strand group comprised of two strands of one color and two strands of another, to produce gradation.
3. Use backstitch for flower stems over leaves.
4. Make plain knots for flowers. Use three colors, as desired, while checking overall color balance.

Freely adapt the leaf, flower, and stem patterns to match your own personal vision.

Refer to p. 62.

Embroidery Position

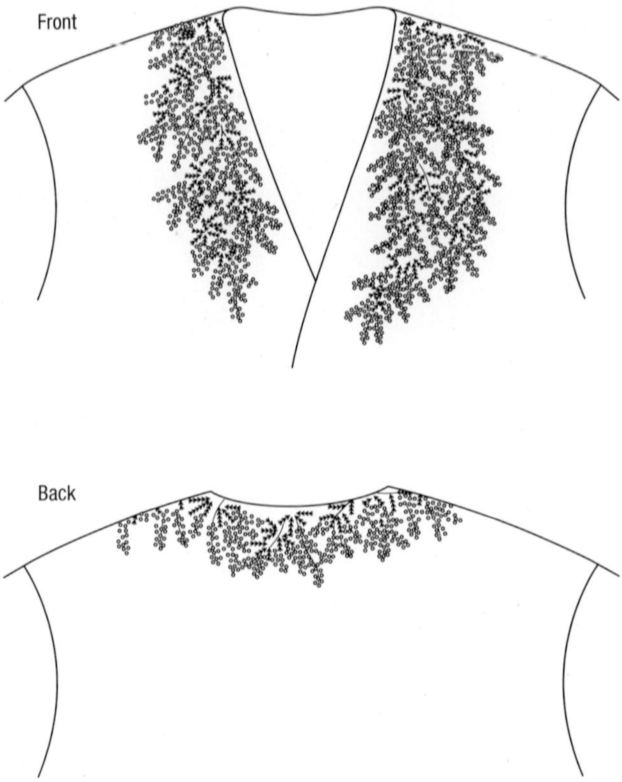

Adapt pattern and embroider on any item you desire.

80% Scale Pattern
Enlarge 80% scale pattern to 125% to produce full-size pattern.

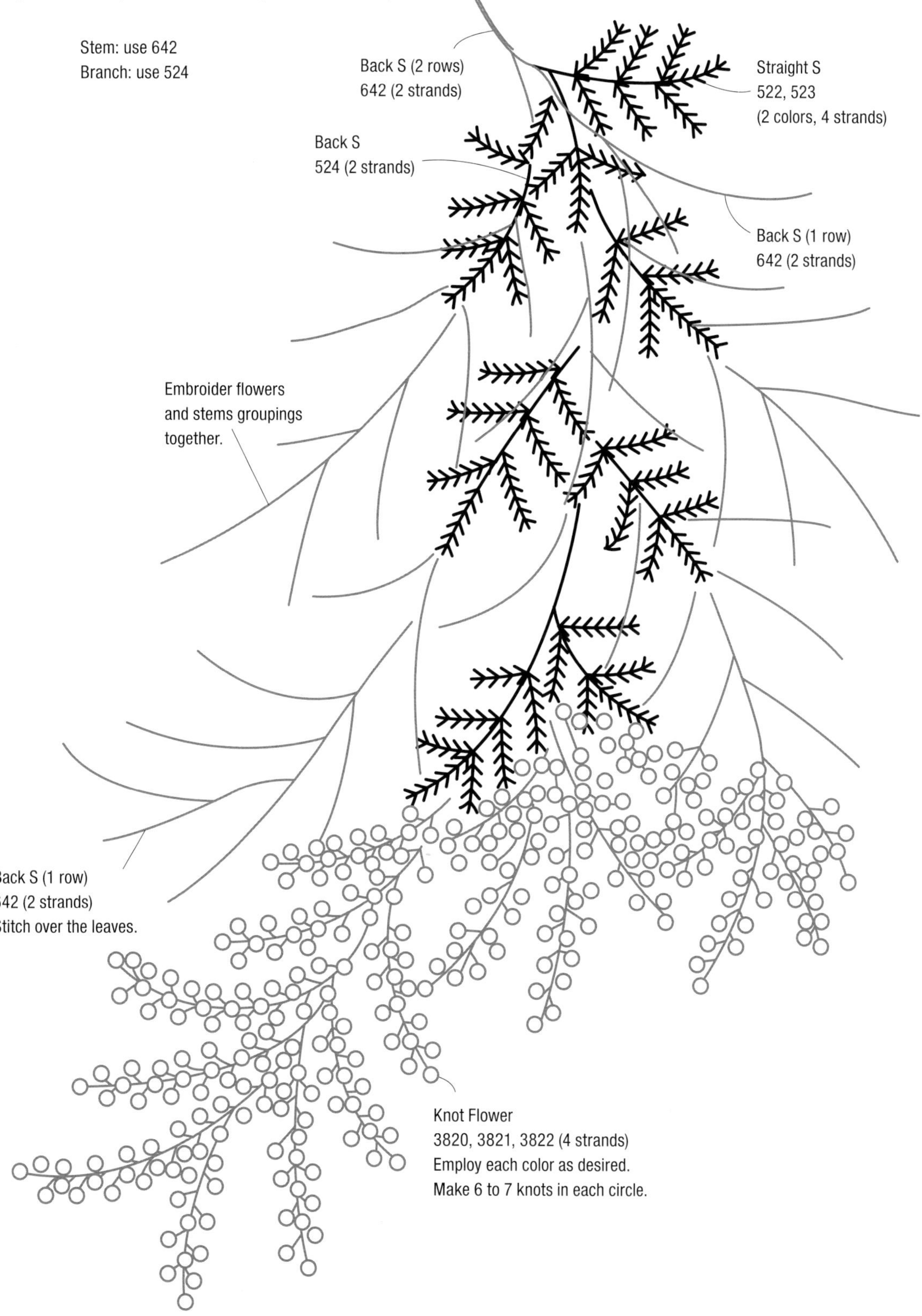

p. 10 Chamomile Drawstring Bag

Finished Size: 20 × 14 cm / 4⅞" × 5½"

⋇ You Will Need

Outer fabric (including bottom) 70 × 30 cm / 27½" × 11¾"

Lining fabric 70 × 25 cm / 27½" × 9⅞"

Fusible interlining 50 × 30 cm / 19¾" × 11¾"

Cord 1 cm / ⅜" wide cotton rope cord 200 cm / 6 9⁄16 ft. long

DMC No. 25 six-stranded Embroidery Floss: 18, 524, 3052, 3348, 3364, 3865

⋇ Notes

- Embroider as desired.
- Instead of stitching the circumference of each cord hole, you can just attach a grommet, if desired. If you choose to stitch around the hole, use a fine blanket stitch around hole circumference.
- Add 1 cm / ⅜" seam allowance. Add 5 cm / 2" seam allowance to the opening on the outer fabric but do not add seam allowance to the opening on the lining fabric.

⋇ Embroidering Instructions

1. Use satin stitch for petals. Use turkey rug stitch for flower center, moving along outline from outside to inside. Cut loops and trim floss short.
2. Work calyx pieces, using long and short stitches in a radial pattern, and adjust edges to blend neatly with petals. Where necessary, combine two strands of single-color floss and two strands of different-colored floss to produce gradation.
3. Use outline stitch for stems.
4. Use satin stitch for scattered petals. Then, straight-stitch petal base.

⋇ Sewing Instructions

1. Embroider outer fabric as desired. Then, fuse interlining to wrong side.
2. Fold outer fabric in half with right side together. Sew the side seam.
3. With right side facing in, sew bottom to outer fabric.
4. Sew lining fabric in the same manner.
5. Insert the lining into outer fabric and fold down seam allowance, on outer fabric, along opening. Sew around top edge.
6. Punch holes at marked positions, then stitch circumference of each hole.
7. Thread cord through each hole and tie loose ends at front.

Outer Fabric: 1 piece
Lining Fabric: 1 piece

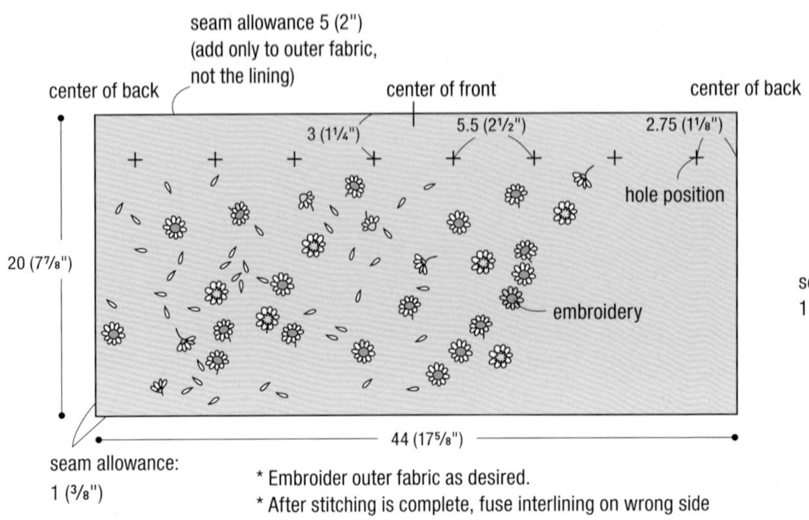

* Embroider outer fabric as desired.
* After stitching is complete, fuse interlining on wrong side of outer fabric.

Bottom: 1 piece
Lining Bottom: 1 piece

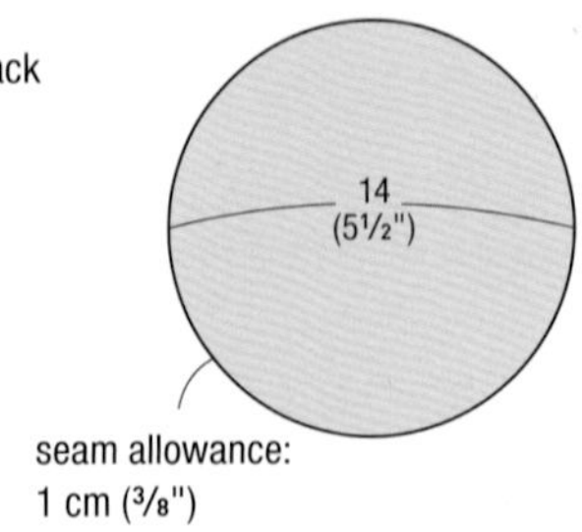

Steps

1

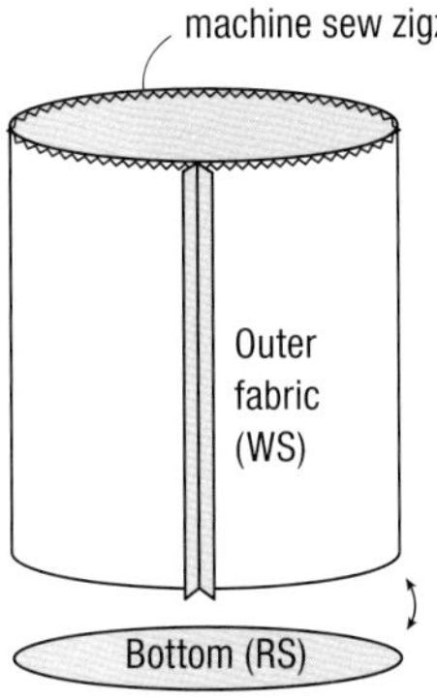

Fold outer fabric in half with right side facing in. Sew side seam. Add zigzag stitch around top edge. With right side facing inward, sew bottom onto outer fabric. Do the same for the lining.

2

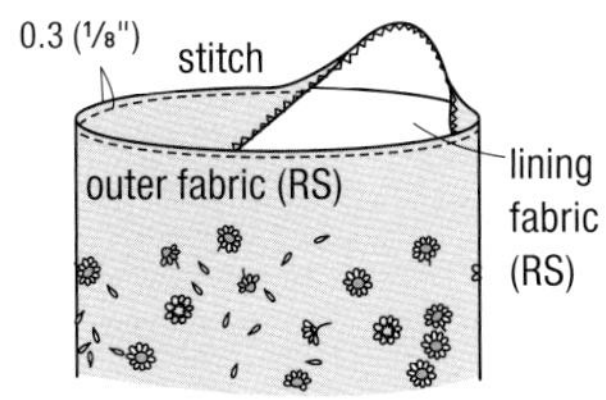

Turn right side out and put lining inside outer fabric. Fold down seam allowance along top edge and sew.

3

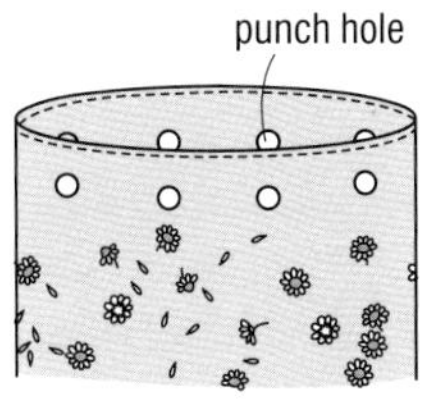

Punch holes based on size of cord. Buttonhole stitch the circumference of each hole.

4

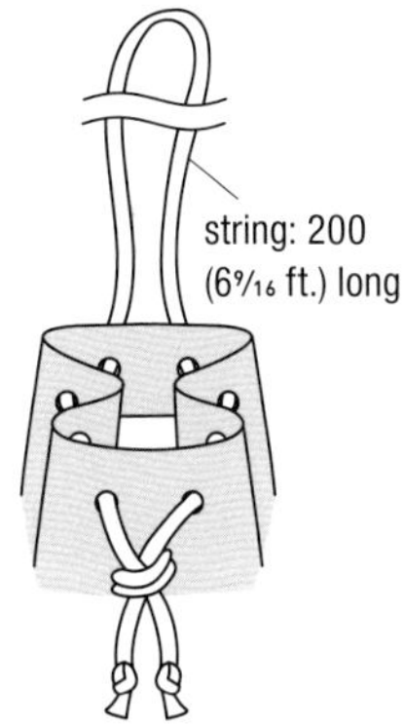

Thread cord through holes and tie loose cord ends together at front.

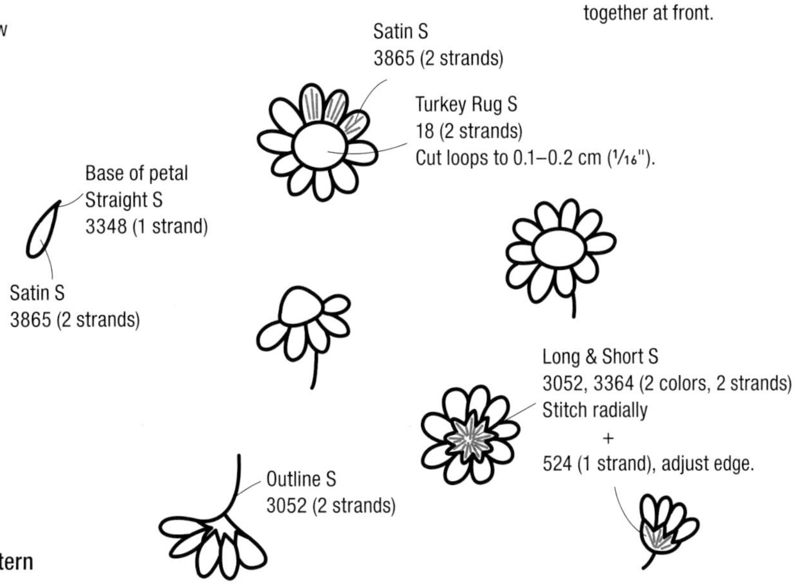

Full-Size Pattern

p. 12 Flowers on Pocket

Full-Size Pattern

❋ Embroidering Instructions

1. Use outline stitch for stems.
2. Use satin stitch and long & short stitch for leaves. Keep stitches close together to fill gaps between stitches.
3. Use turkey rug stitch to make petals. Stitch two rows. Begin with outside petals. Stitch second row at base of first row. Use French knot stitch for flower centers at base of second turkey rug stitch row. Overlapping with the first row, use long & short stitch for base of second row of sside-facing flowers.
4. Use long & short stitch for calyx.

Refer to p. 64.

Embroidery Position

Adapt pattern and embroider on any item you desire.

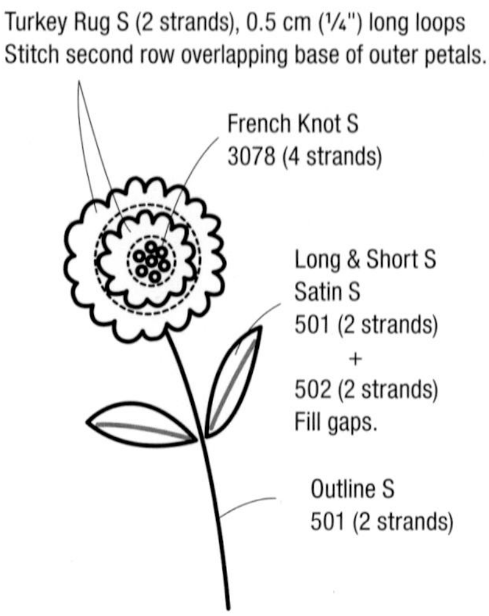

Full-Size Pattern

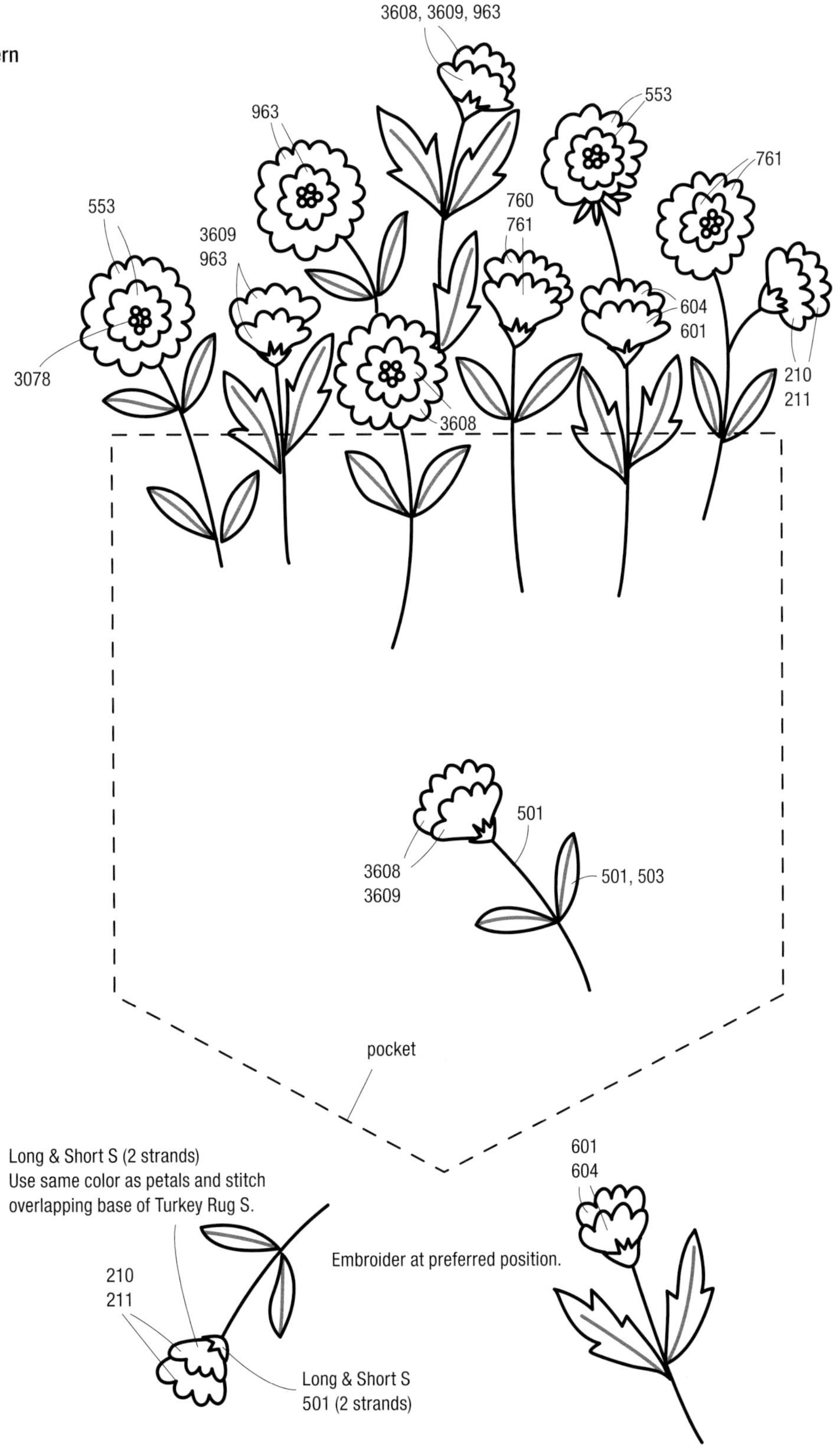

p. 14 Dandelion

80% Scale Pattern.   Enlarge 80% scale pattern to 125% to produce full-size pattern.

※ Embroidering Instructions

- Use satin stitch for stems and roots. Adjust length of roots as desired.
- Use long & short stitches for leaves. Fill gaps between stitches to cover areas fully.
- Use satin stitch for calyx and produce shading as for the leaves.
- Use satin stitch for each petal. Use turkey rug stitch for flower center and leave loops 0.4–0.5 cm / ⅛" long. Use French knot stitch for flower center on inside of the turkey rug stitch on rightmost flower.
- Use satin stitch and straight stitch for dandelion puffs. Stitch outermost puffs first, making a circular outline, and then begin to fill. Stitch over the calyx and seeds.
- Use satin stitch for bud. Then, outline stitch to add patterns.

Refer to pp. 63, 64.

Where necessary, combine two strands of single-color floss and two strands of different-colored floss to produce gradation.

Embroidery Position

Adapt pattern and embroider on any item you desire.

80% Scale Pattern
Enlarge 80% scale pattern to 125% to produce full-size pattern.

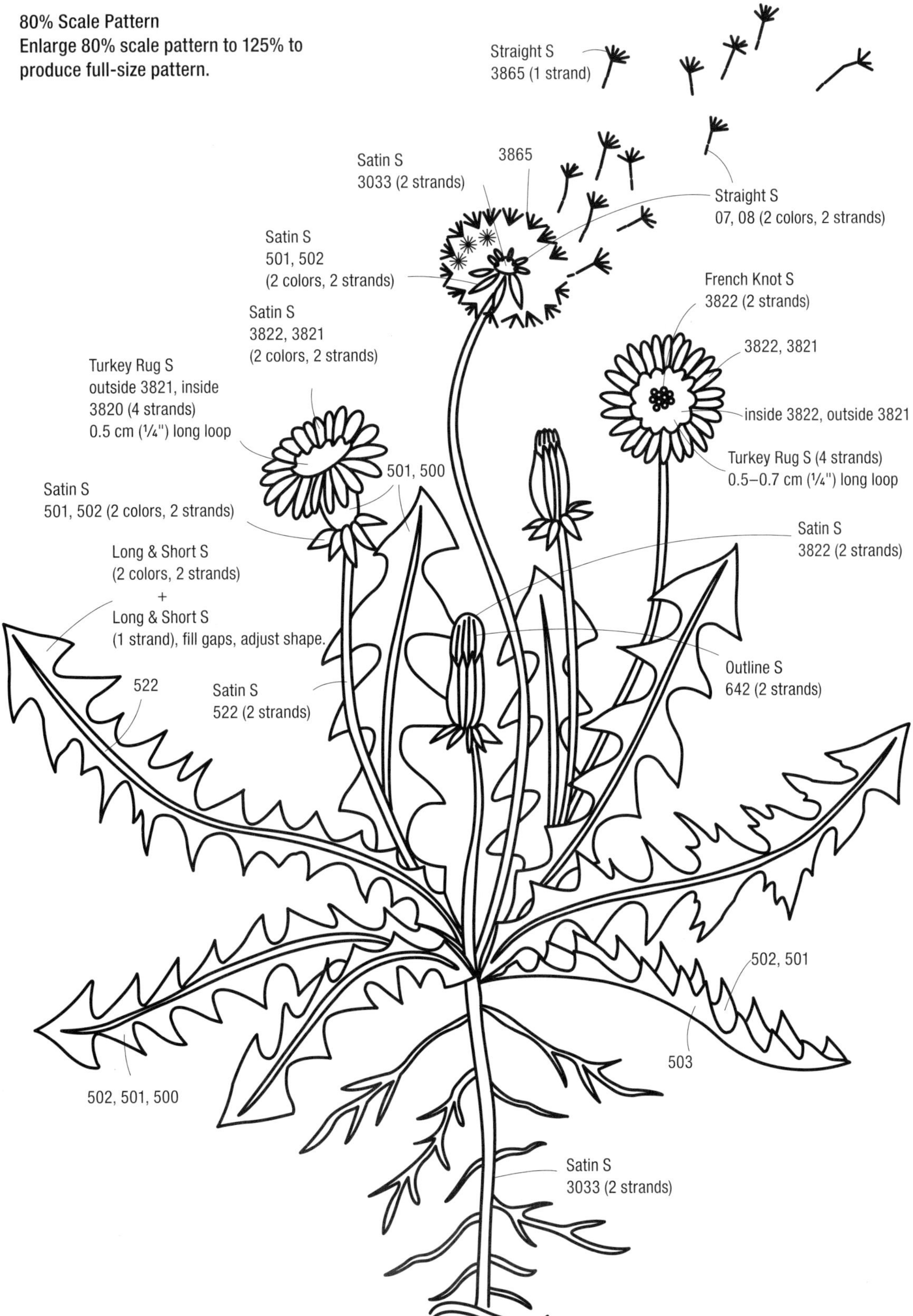

p. 16 Spring Flowers Bag

Finished Size: 32 × 40 cm / 12⅝" × 15¾"

⋇ You Will Need

Outer fabric 50 × 70 cm / 19¾" × 27½"

Lining fabric (includes pockets) 70 × 70 cm / 27½" × 27½"

20 cm / 7⅞" long zipper 1pc.

3 cm / 1⅛" wide, 85 cm / 33½" long flat cord

A pair of 2 cm / ¾" diameter sew-on snap fasteners

DMC No. 25 six-stranded embroidery floss: ECRU, 151, 159, 209, 210, 211, 225, 341, 524, 677, 3052, 3053, 3348, 3354, 3363, 3364, 3733, 3752, 3753, 3790, 3822, 3865

⋇ Notes

- Add 1 cm / ⅜" seam allowance.
- Use thick fabric for lining.

⋇ Embroidering Instructions

- Use long & short stitch for petals. Keep stitches close together to fill areas. Further fill gaps between stitches while making a neat outline of the flower. Last, stitch flower center and its patterns.
- Refer to p. 68 for chamomile flowers.
- After using satin stitching for muscari flowers—in a circular shape—make French knot stitches to add frills to bottom flower tiers.
- Randomly employ long & short stitch for leaves and calyx, while keeping in mind the gradation. Fill gaps between stitches to fill areas.
- Randomly employ long & short stitch for leaves on the Persian buttercup, keeping an eye on the colors.
- Combine outline stitches and straight stitches for the chamomile leaves.
- Make two or three rows of outline stitches to create thicker stem portions and then fill gaps between rows with single-strand outline stitches.
- Use two strands of two different-colored pieces of floss to create stems of muscari and Persian buttercups.

Refer to pp. 62, 63.

Where necessary, combine two strands of single-color floss and two strands of different-colored floss to gradate.

⋇ Sewing Instructions

1. Embroider on outer fabric.
2. Fold outer fabric in half with right side facing in. Sew both side seams.
3. Make inside pockets and attach them to the lining fabric.
4. Sew lining fabric in same manner as outer fabric.
5. Put outer fabric inside lining, right side in, and sew along top edge.
6. Turn right side out, stitch along top edge.
7. Attach a snap fastener and handle.

Inside Pocket A: 1 piece

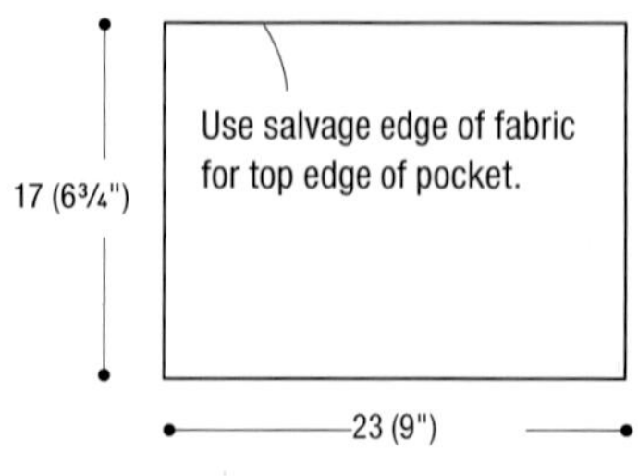

Inside Pocket B Top: 1 piece

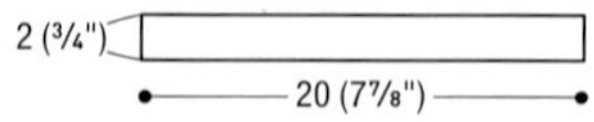

Inside Pocket B Bottom: 1 piece

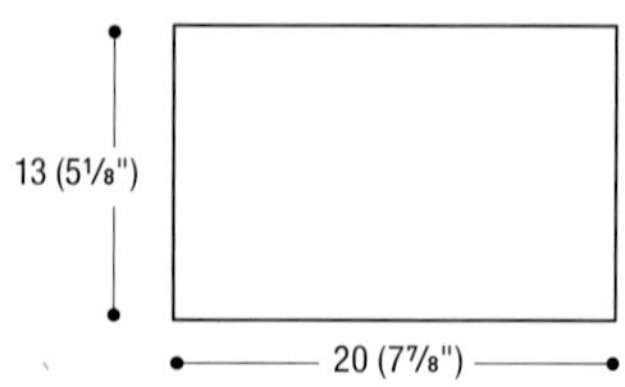

How to Sew Inside Pocket B

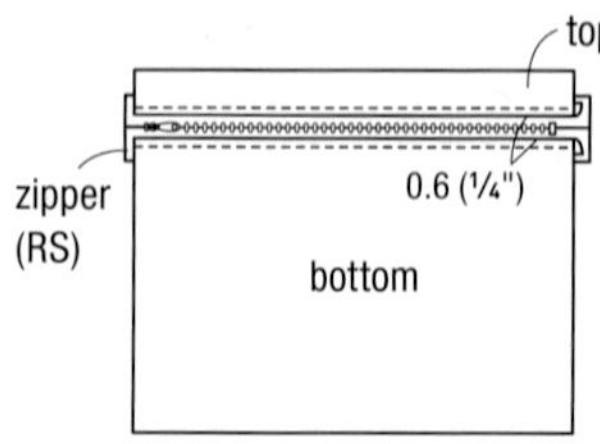

Install zipper to top and bottom piece.

Outer Fabric: 1 piece

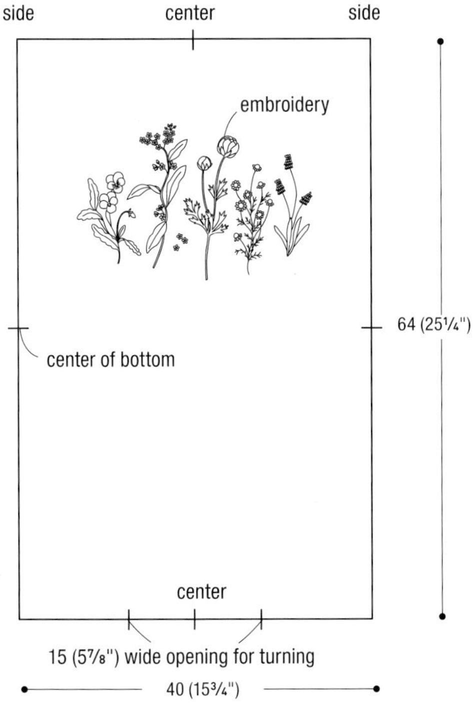

Lining Fabric: 1 piece

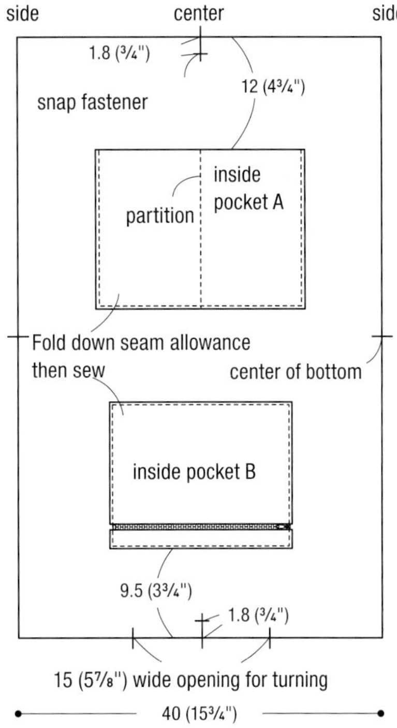

Steps

1

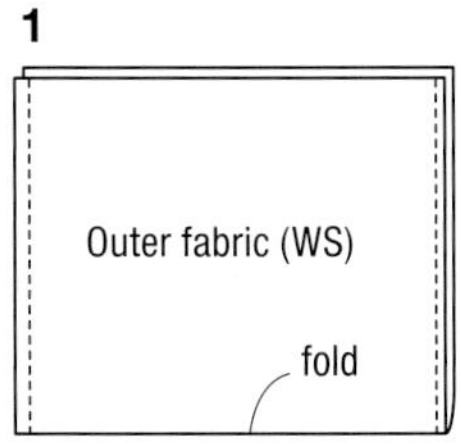

Fold in half, right side in. Sew both side seams.
Do the same for lining fabric.

2

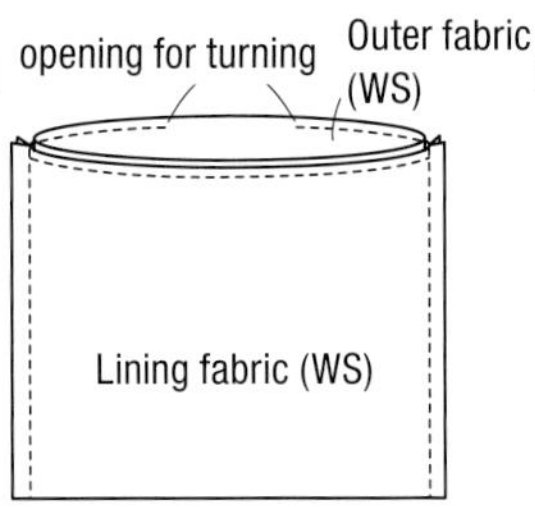

Put outer fabric inside lining fabric, right sides together.
Sew along top edge, leaving an opening for turning.

3

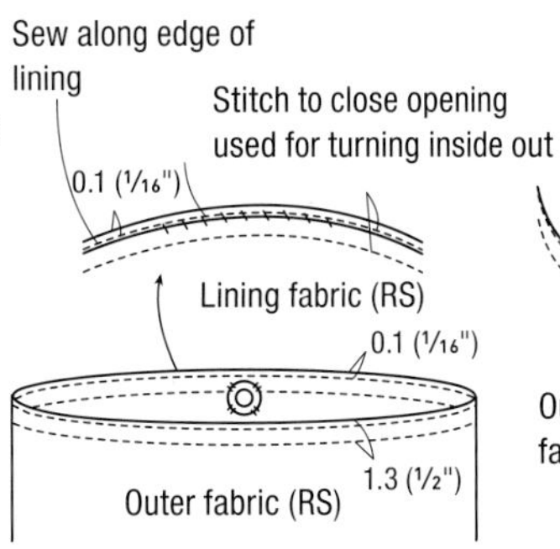

Turn right side out, close opening used for turning inside out.
Stitch along top edge.
Attach snap fastener.

4

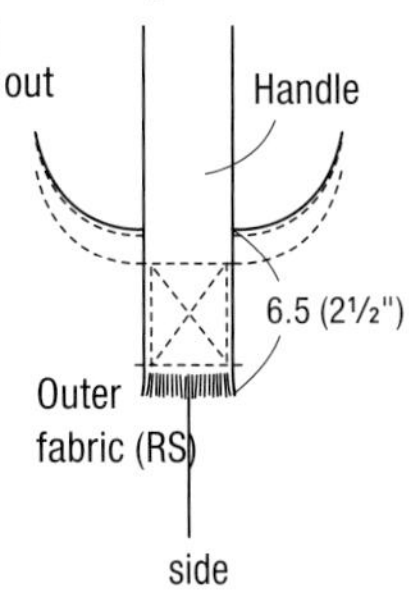

Sew on handle.

Full-Size Pattern

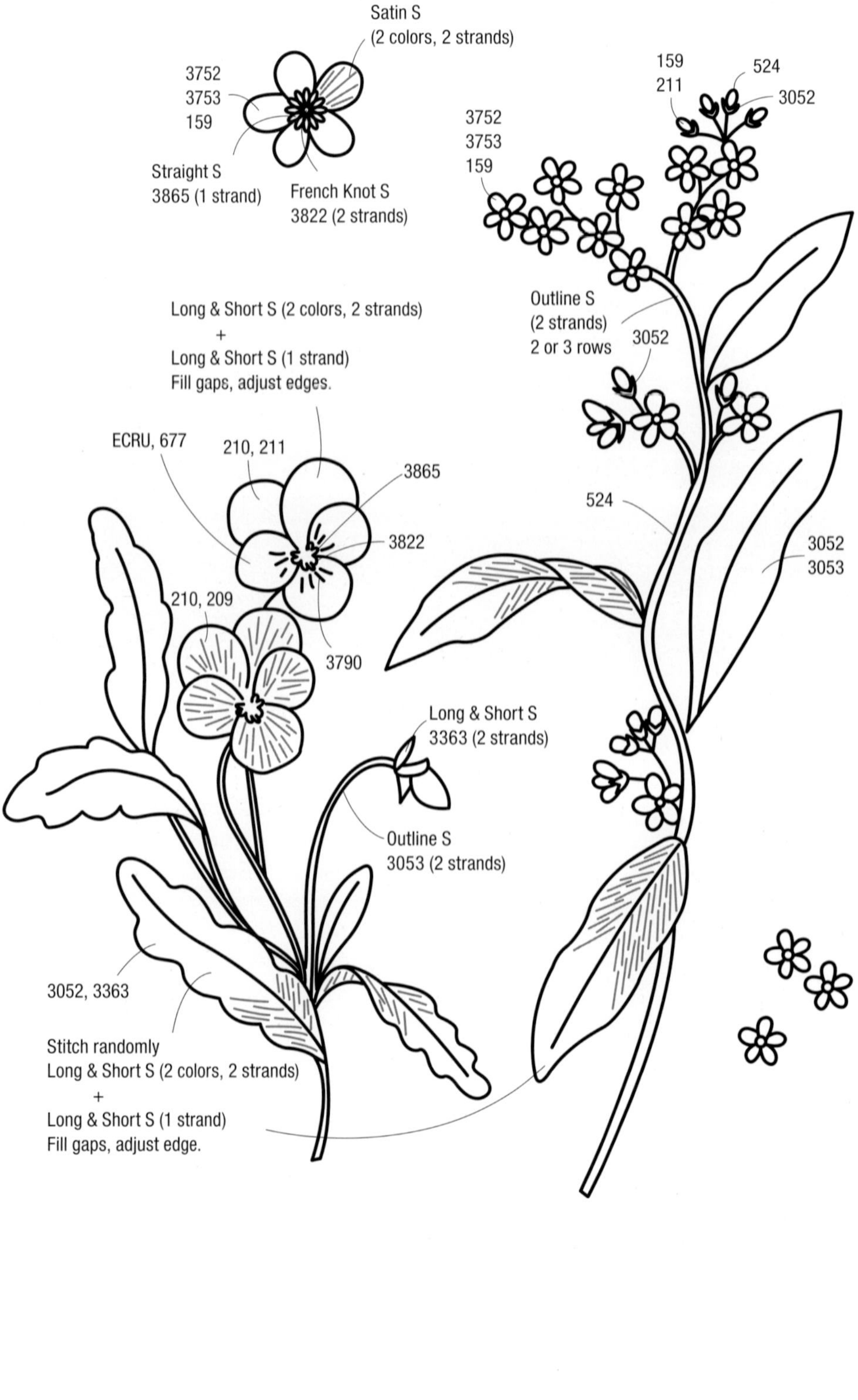

Full-Size Pattern

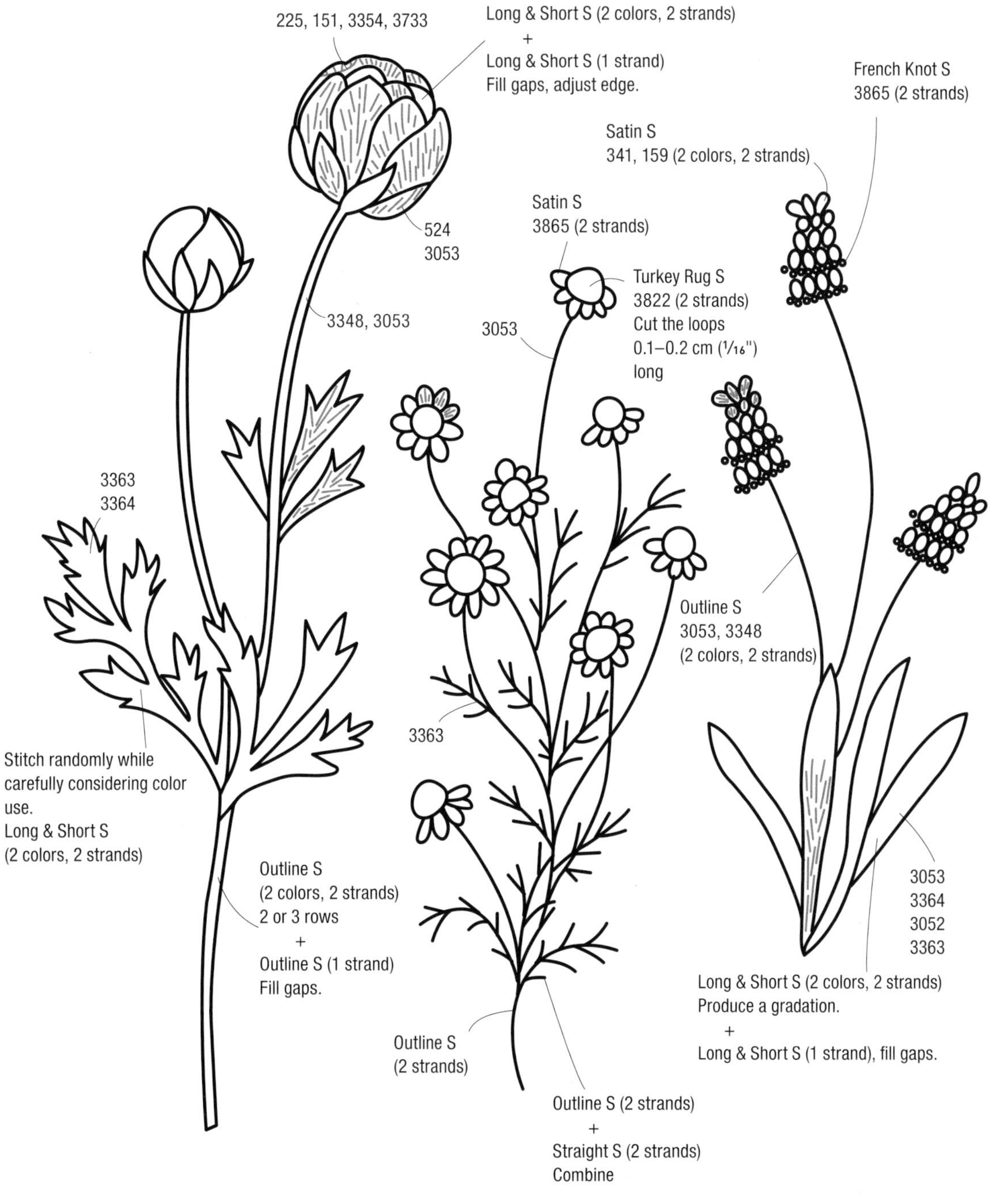

p. 18 Dried-Flower Purse

Finished Size A • B 7.5 × 8.5 cm / 3" × 3⅜", C 10 × 9 cm / 4" × 3½"

⁂ You Will Need

A • B Common: Outer fabric, Lining fabric, Fusible interlining 30 × 15 cm / 11¾" × 5⅞"

One metal purse frame: dimension 6.9 × 4 cm / 2¾" × 1⅝"

DMC No. 25 six-stranded embroidery floss A:422, 642, 644, 648, 738, 739, 3790

B: ECRU, 932, 3753, 3756

C: Outer fabric, Lining fabric, Fusible interlining 30 × 15 cm / 11¾" × 5⅞"

One metal purse frame: dimension 7.5 × 3.8 cm / 3" × 1½"

DMC No. 25 six-stranded embroidery floss: ECRU, 224, 225, 523, 524, 642, 738, 739, 3022

⁂ Note

- Add 1 cm / ⅜" seam allowance.

⁂ Embroidering Instructions

- Refer to pattern on p. 80 for embroidered design.

⁂ Sewing Instructions

1. Embroider on front outer fabric and fuse interlining on wrong side.
2. Lay front outer fabric flat, with right sides together, on back outer fabric. Sew both side seams, bottom, and boxed corners.
3. Sew lining fabric in the same manner as outer fabric.
4. Put outer fabric inside lining fabric, right sides together, and sew along top edge. Leave an opening for turning.
5. Turn right side out and attach metal purse frame.

A

B

C

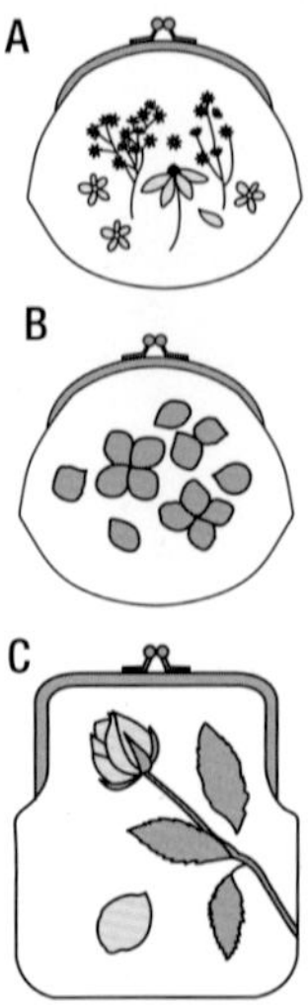

A Outer Fabric Front: 1 piece **B Outer Fabric Front: 1 piece**

AB Common

Outer Fabric Back: 1 piece
Lining Fabric: 2 pieces

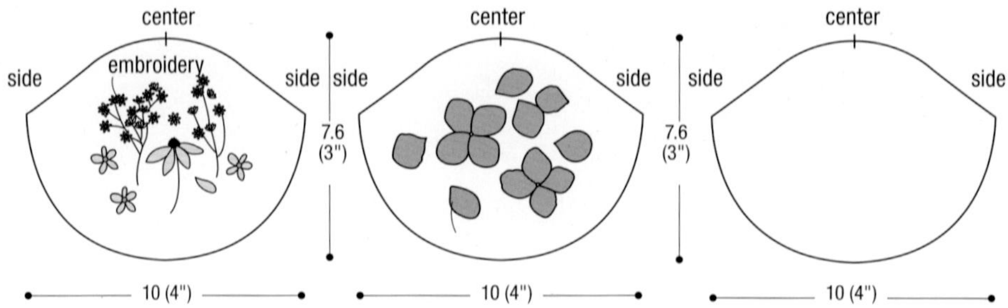

* After stitching is complete, fuse interlining on wrong side of outer fabric.

C Outer Fabric Front: 1 piece

Outer Fabric Back: 1 piece
Lining Fabric: 2 pieces

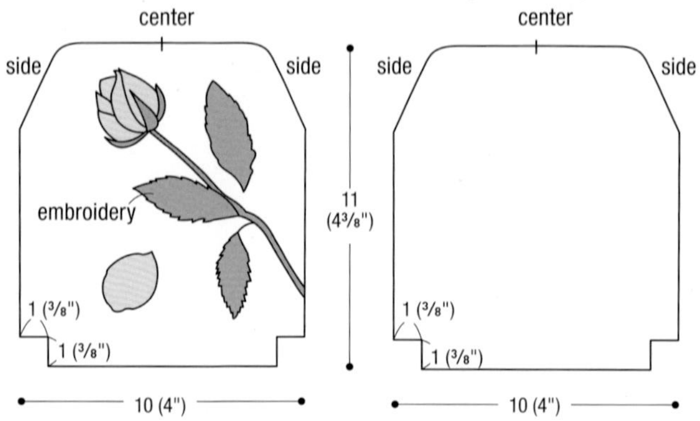

* After stitching is complete, fuse interlining on wrong side of outer fabric.

Steps

1

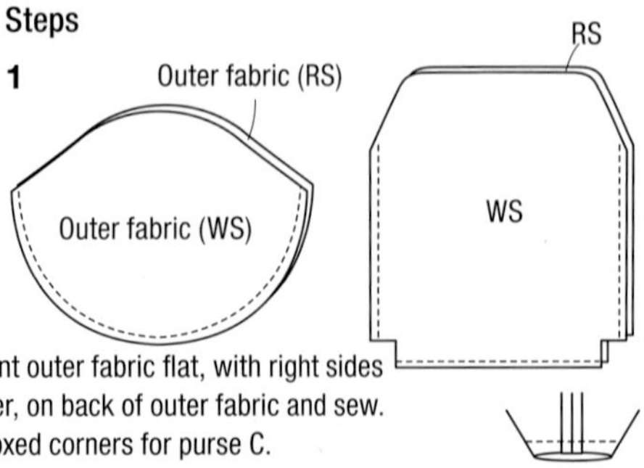

Lay front outer fabric flat, with right sides together, on back of outer fabric and sew. Sew boxed corners for purse C. Do the same for the lining fabric.

2

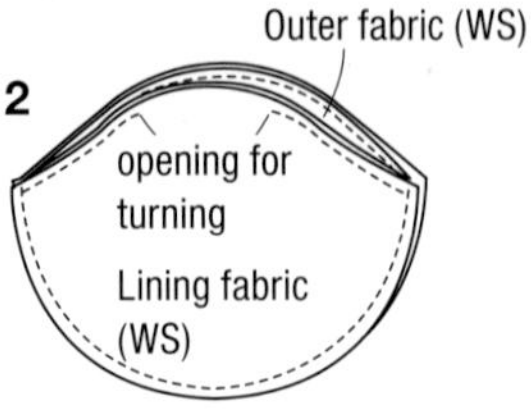

Put outer fabric inside lining fabric, with right sides together. Sew along top edge. Leave an opening for turning.

3

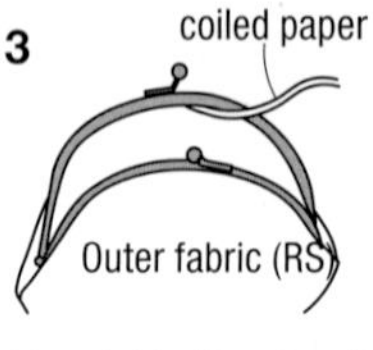

Turn right side out and adjust the seam allowance on the opening for turning. Attach metal purse frame.

Full-Size Pattern

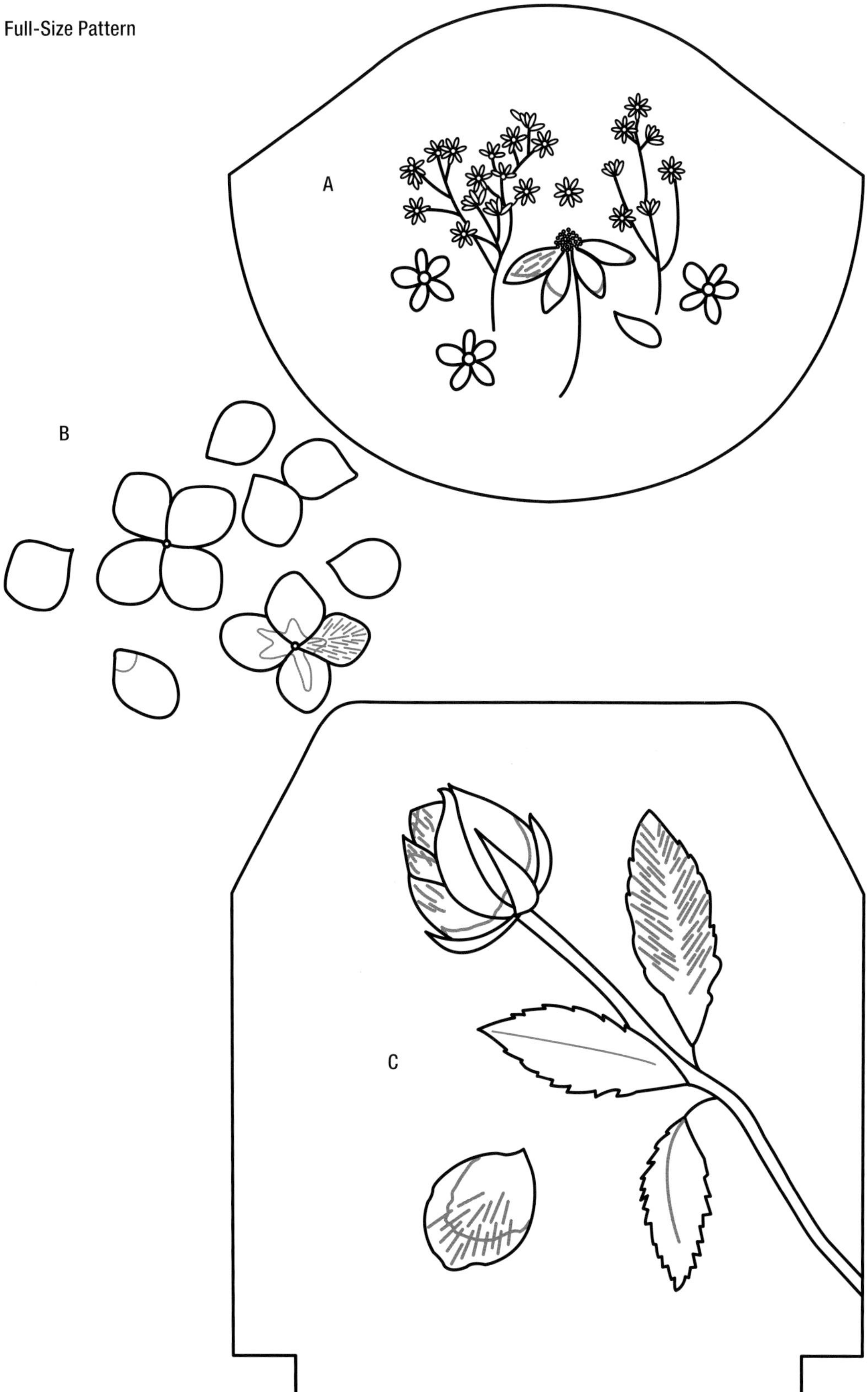

p. 20 Dried Flowers

Full-Size Pattern

※ Embroidering Instructions

- Use long & short stitch for large petals and to fill area. Further, fill gaps between stitches. Adjust edge, using single strand of embroidery floss.
- Use satin stitch for small petals and make French knots at flower center. Tie knots with embroidery floss several times at marked spots to make mimosa flowers.
- Use long & short stitch for large leaves and calyx, while keeping in mind the desired gradation. Fill gaps between stitches to fill in areas.
- Use two strands of embroidery floss and straight stitch to make the mimosa leaves. Use outline stitch for the chamomile leaves. Then, stitch using single strand of embroidery floss to adjust the shape.
- Use backstitch or outline stitch for stems. Make two to three rows of your chosen stitch to create thick portions of the stems.

Refer to pp. 62, 63.

Where necessary, combine two strands of single-color floss and two strands of different-colored floss to produce gradation.

Full-Size Pattern

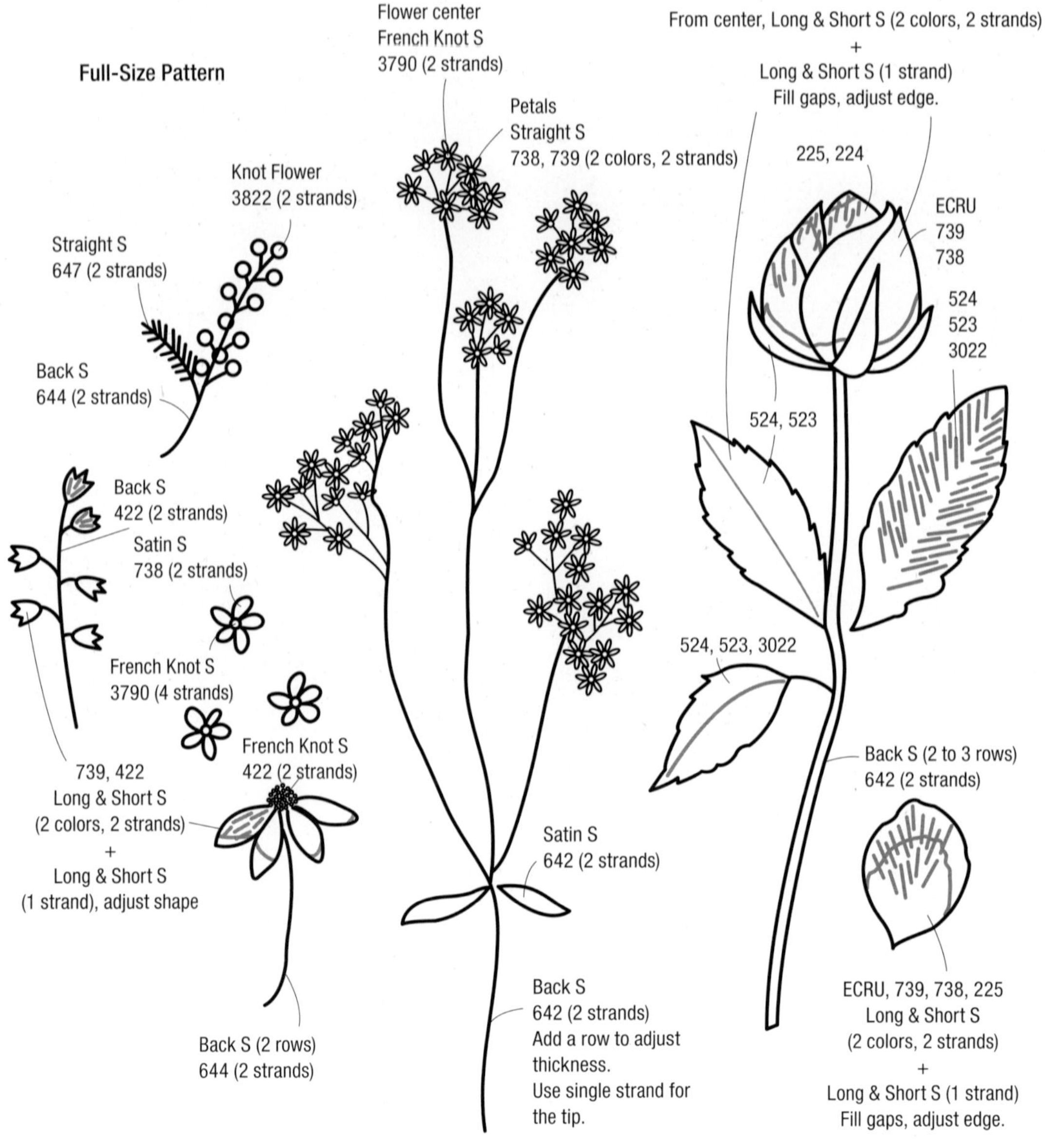

Full-Size Pattern

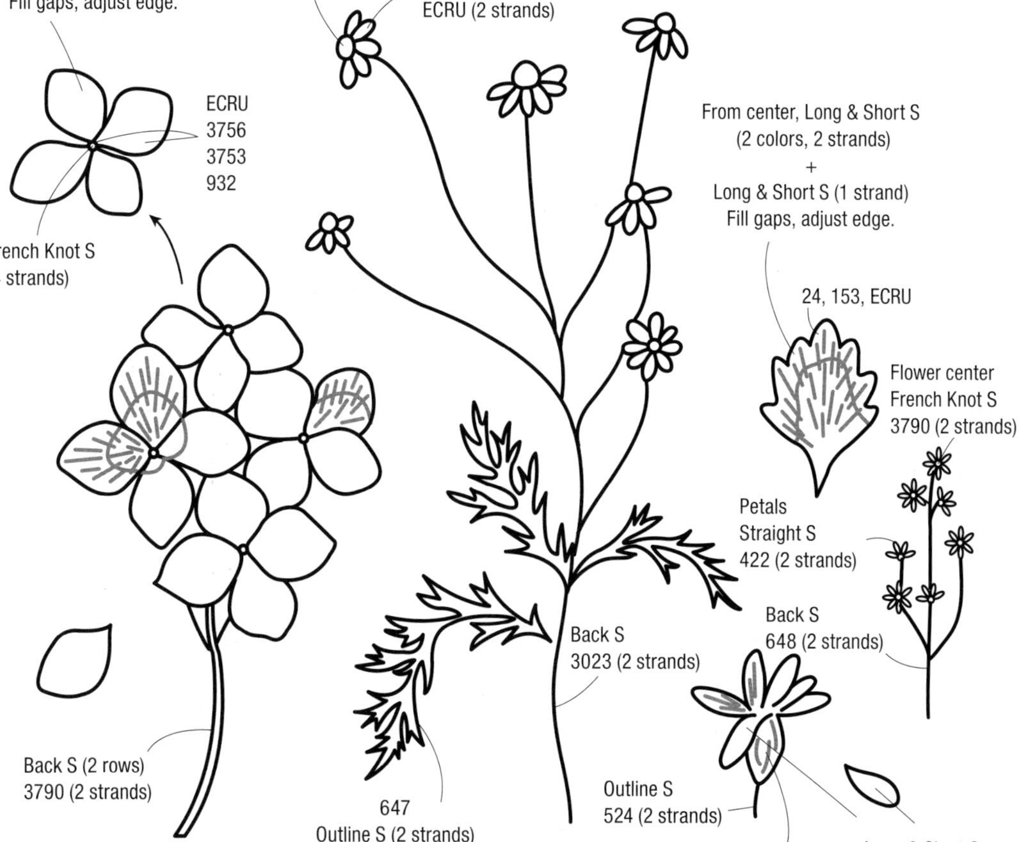

p. 6 Many Flowers

Full-Size Pattern

❋ Embroidering Instructions

Mimosa: Refer to pp. 62, 66. Petals: Refer to pp. 63, 74. Chamomile: Refer to pp. 68. Also refer to pp. 74, 80 for other flowers. Feel free to incorporate flowers from other pages in this book.

Where necessary, combine two strands (or four strands) of single-color floss and two strands (or four strands) of different-colored floss to produce gradation.

Scabiosa

1. Use long & short stitch for petals and to fill. Work further to tightly fill area and adjust shape. Use single-strand floss to neatly adjust the outline.
2. Make turkey rug stitches that encircle flower center.
3. Stitch stamens. Tie knot in floss tail and secure between turkey rug stitch.
4. Stitch pistil. Fill center with French knots.

White Flower

1. Use satin stitch for petals.
2. Use French knot stitch for flower center.

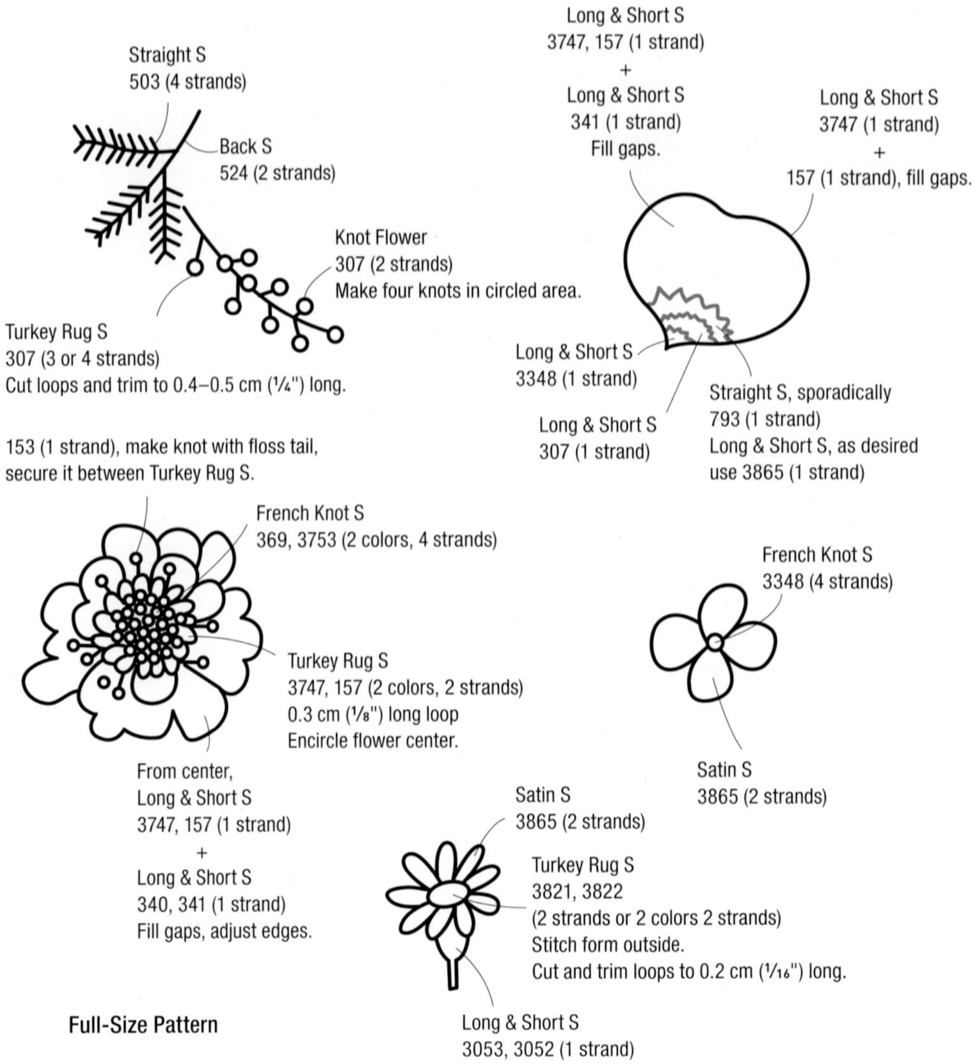

p. 22 Butterfly Envelope-Shaped Pouch

Finished Size: 13.5 × 20 cm / 5¼" × 7⅞"

⋇ You Will Need

Outer fabric, inner fabric, fusible interfacing 25 × 40 cm / 9⅞" × 15¾"

A pair of 0.7 cm / ¼" diameter sew-on snap fasteners

DMC No. 25 six-stranded embroidery floss A: ECRU, 02, 209, 211, 307, 310, 340, 341, 347, 445, 524, 597, 598, 648, 727, 739, 746, 823, 844, 3031, 3052, 3053, 3078, 3348, 3782, 3839, 3840, 3865

B: ECRU, 3031, 3782, 3790

⋇ Note

- Add 1 cm / ⅜" seam allowance.

⋇ Embroidering Instructions

- Pouch A—Butterfly: Make long & short stitches to fill area while mixing different-colored floss. Pouch B—Butterfly: Use outline stitch around butterfly border without filling area. Where necessary, combine two strands of single-color floss and two strands of different-colored floss to produce gradation.
- Feel free to refer to instructions on pp. 76 and 80 for the flowers in this work.

⋇ Sewing Instructions

1. After stitching is complete, fuse interlining to wrong side of fabric.
2. Align outer and inner fabric, right sides together, sew top edge (angled).
3. With the right side facing up, fold along center of bottom and sew both side seams. Then, flap while leaving an opening for turning.
4. Turn right side out and close opening.
5. Attach a snap fastener.

A

B

* After stitching is complete, fuse interlining on wrong side.

A Outer Fabric: 1 piece

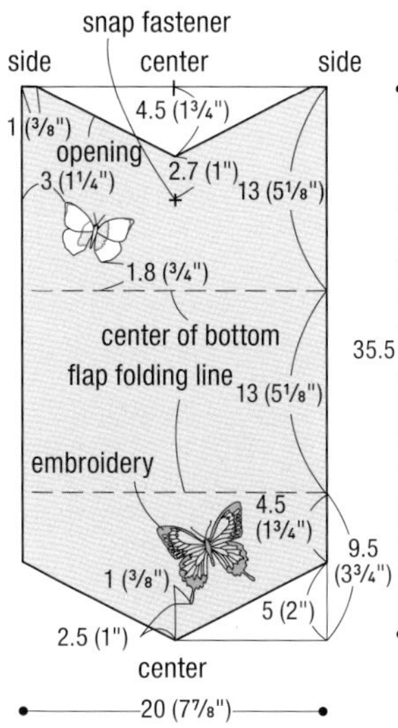

A Inner Fabric: 1 piece

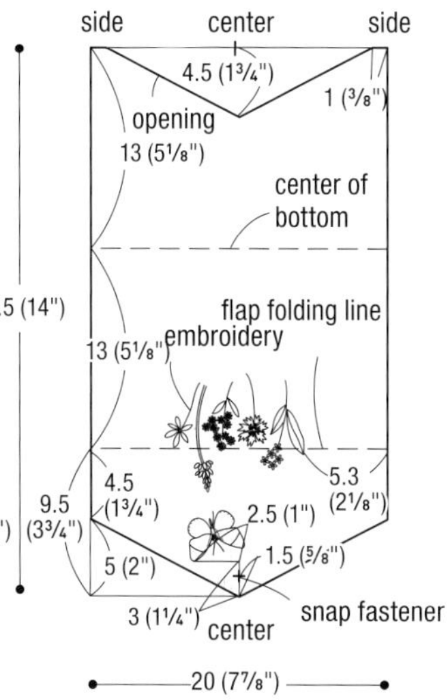

Steps

1

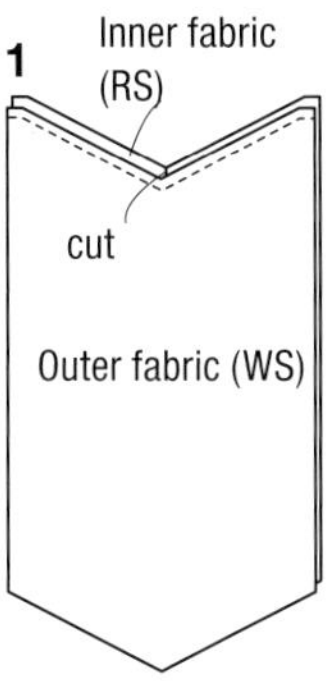

Align outer and inner fabric, right sides together, and sew reverse V-shaped edge.

2

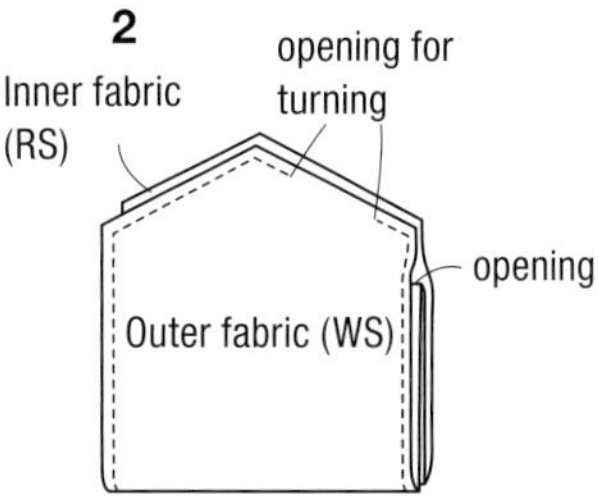

Fold along center of bottom and sew, except opening for turning.

3

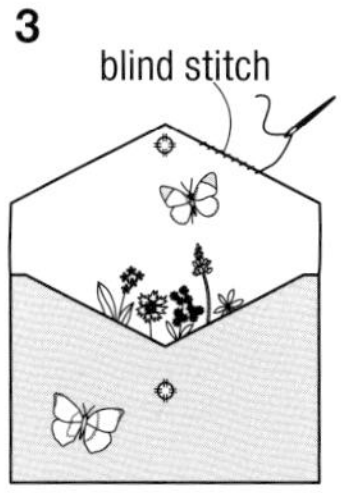

Turn right side out and close the opening. Attach a snap fastener.

B Outer Fabric: 1 piece

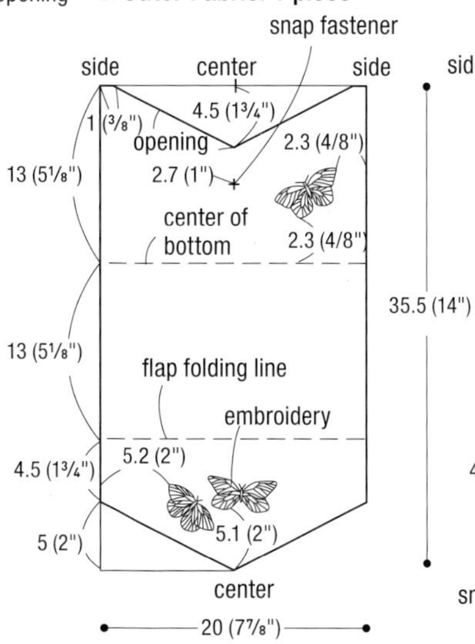

B Inner Fabric: 1 piece

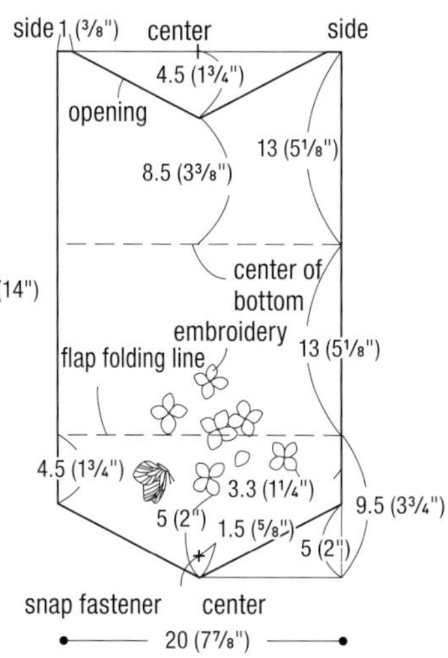

* After stitching is complete, fuse interlining on wrong side.

Full-Size Pattern

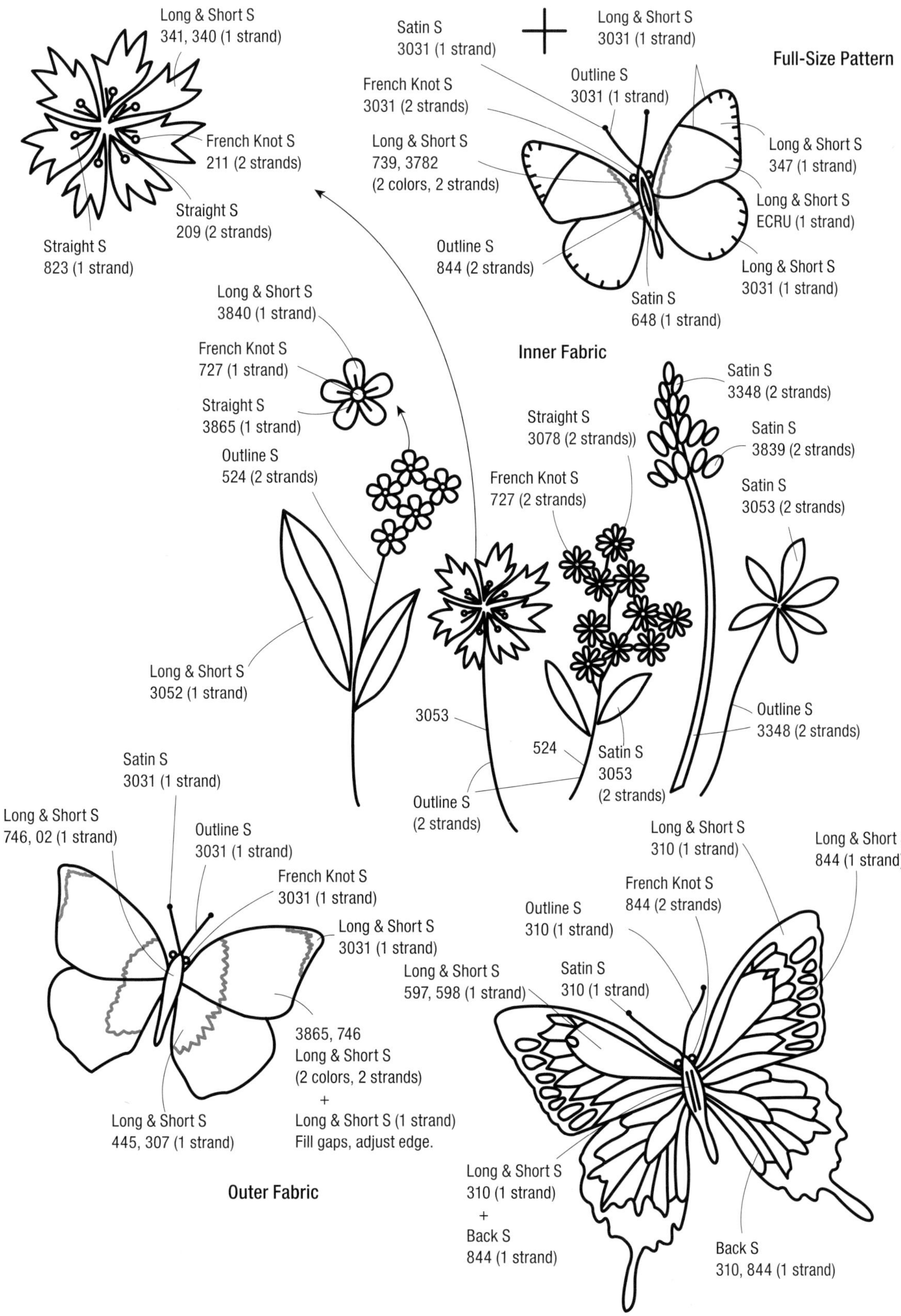
Full-Size Pattern
Satin S
3031 (1 strand)
Long & Short S
3031 (1 strand)
Outline S
3031 (1 strand)
French Knot S
3031 (2 strands)
Long & Short S
739, 3782
(2 colors, 2 strands)
Long & Short S
347 (1 strand)
Long & Short S
ECRU (1 strand)
Outline S
844 (2 strands)
Long & Short S
3031 (1 strand)
Satin S
648 (1 strand)
Long & Short S
341, 340 (1 strand)
French Knot S
211 (2 strands)
Straight S
209 (2 strands)
Straight S
823 (1 strand)
Long & Short S
3840 (1 strand)
French Knot S
727 (1 strand)
Straight S
3865 (1 strand)
Outline S
524 (2 strands)
Inner Fabric
Satin S
3348 (2 strands)
Straight S
3078 (2 strands))
Satin S
3839 (2 strands)
French Knot S
727 (2 strands)
Satin S
3053 (2 strands)
Long & Short S
3052 (1 strand)
3053
Outline S
3348 (2 strands)
524
Satin S
3053
(2 strands)
Outline S
(2 strands)
Satin S
3031 (1 strand)
Long & Short S
746, 02 (1 strand)
Outline S
3031 (1 strand)
French Knot S
3031 (1 strand)
Long & Short S
3031 (1 strand)
3865, 746
Long & Short S
(2 colors, 2 strands)
+
Long & Short S (1 strand)
Fill gaps, adjust edge.
Long & Short S
445, 307 (1 strand)
Outer Fabric
Long & Short S
310 (1 strand)
Long & Short S
844 (1 strand)
French Knot S
844 (2 strands)
Outline S
310 (1 strand)
Satin S
310 (1 strand)
Long & Short S
597, 598 (1 strand)
Long & Short S
310 (1 strand)
+
Back S
844 (1 strand)
Back S
310, 844 (1 strand)

p. 24 Polar Bear, Hedgehog, Donkey, Fox

Full-Size Pattern

⋇ Embroidering Instructions: Polar Bear

1. Stitch face and paws. Face and paws: Long & short stitch. Nose: Satin stitch. Mouth, eyes, and claws: Straight stitch. Leave small borders around turkey rug stitch in face area.
2. Begin turkey rug stitch from tail and paws. Stitch against the flow of fur.
3. After filling body area with turkey rug stitch up to the face, use bullion stitch for ear. Then, make turkey rug stitches that nestle into base of the ear.
4. After making turkey rug stitches up to face and body borders, make long & short stitches that overlap the turkey rug stitches and adjust the look.
5. Cut and trim off turkey rug stitch loops. Vary length to produce a three-dimensional effect on legs.

⋇ Embroidering Instructions: Hedgehog

1. On target material (in this case, a shirt), use turkey rug stitch for spines. Where necessary, combine two strands of single-color floss and two strands of different-colored floss. Cut loops and trim short at top and inside. Make loops longer toward outside.
2. Transfer face position onto patch and use turkey rug stitch for face. Cut loops and trim short near inside of face. Leave slightly longer toward the outside. On top, make eyes and mouth using satin stitch. Make long bullion stitches to create loops for ears.

⋇ How to Make a Hedgehog Pocket

1. Embroider spines on base fabric.
2. Lay pocket fabric on base fabric, right sides together, and sew face outline.
3. Cut out the face. Push pocket fabric through hole to back of base fabric.
4. Bind bottom of hole, using same embroidery floss as the spines. This creates the mouth of the pocket.
5. Lay patch over base fabric, right sides facing up, and mark outline of hole (face). Use this as a guide to stitch facial features.
6. Embroider face on outline marked patch. Use long turkey rug stitches and make lower outline longer than the rest.
7. Sew along face outline, except the area bound in step 4, to connect the three pieces of fabric.
8. Align pocket fabric with the patch and trim off excess. Then, sew sides.

Full-Size Pattern: Polar Bear

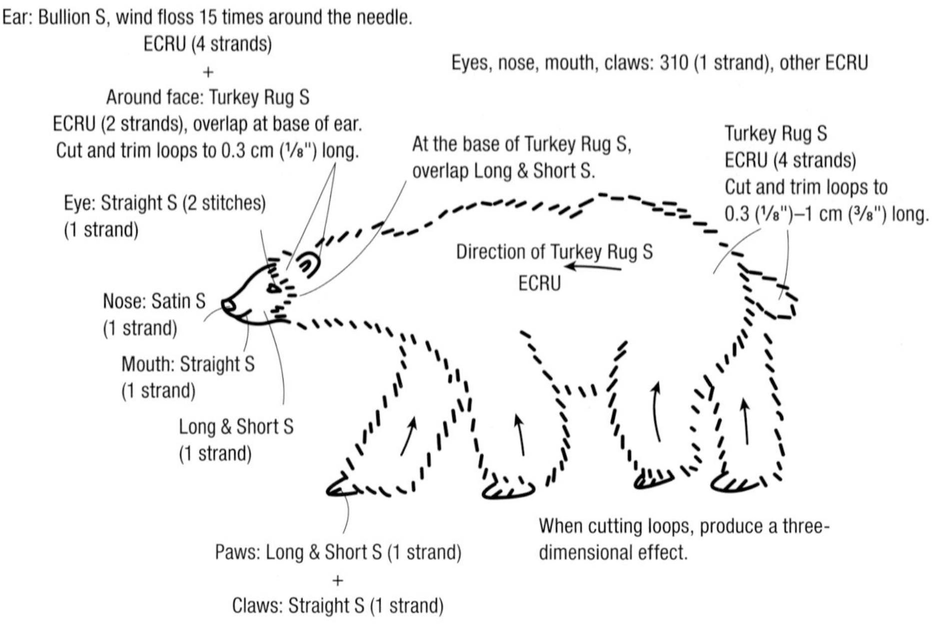

Embroidering Instructions: Hedgehog

1

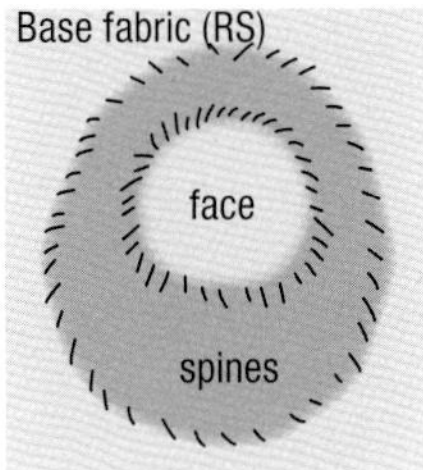

Use Turkey rug stitch for spines while leaving the face alone.

2

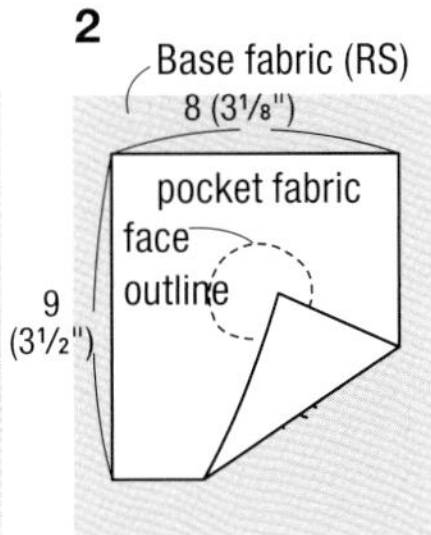

Lay pocket fabric on base fabric, right sides together, and sew outline of face.

3

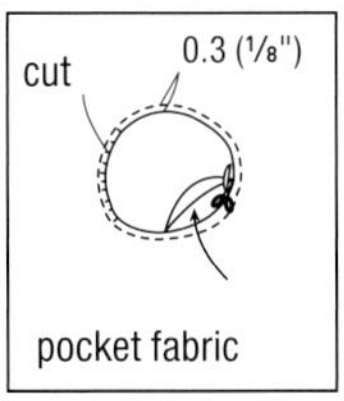

Cut inside stitched line and push pocket fabric through the hole.

4

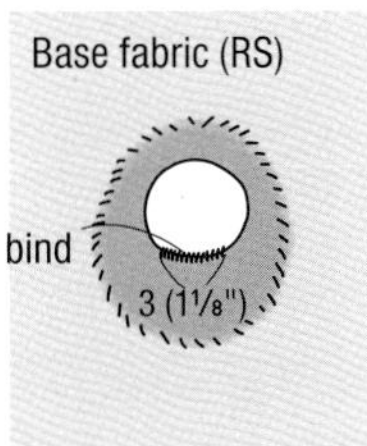

Bind bottom of hole

5

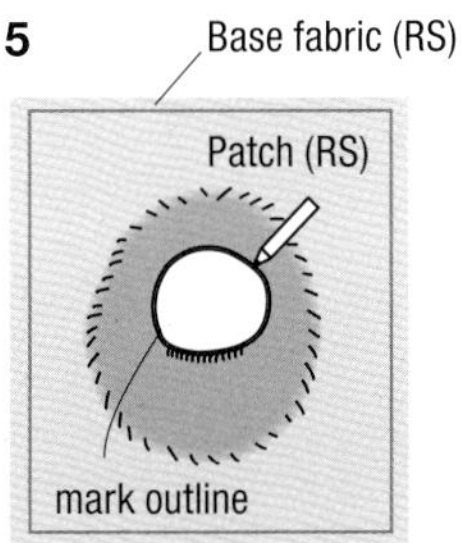

Put another piece of patch under base fabric and mark face position.

6

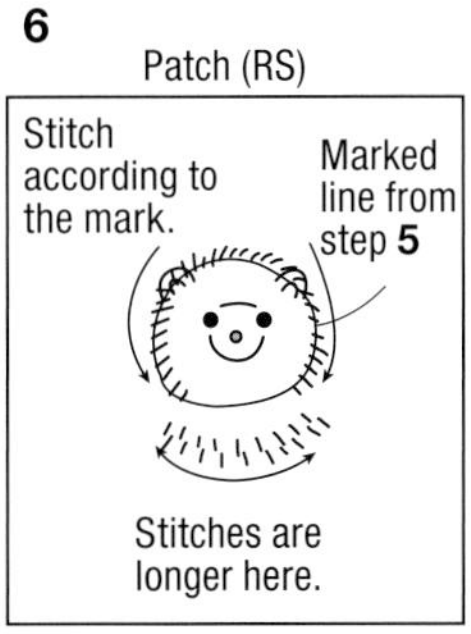

Embroider face on patch.

7

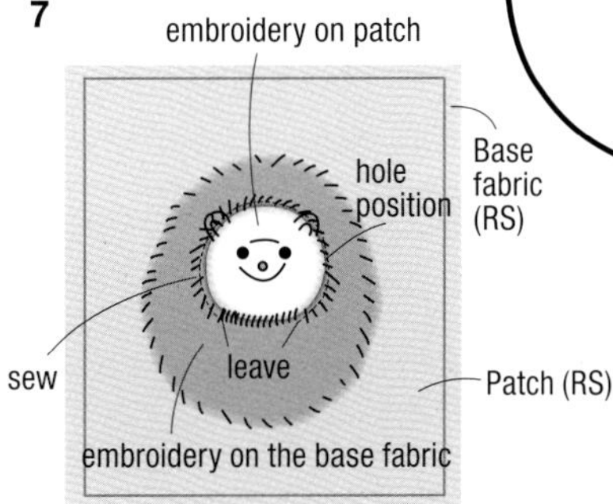

Align patch with back of base fabric and match face to spines.
Sew along face outline, except where already bound.

8

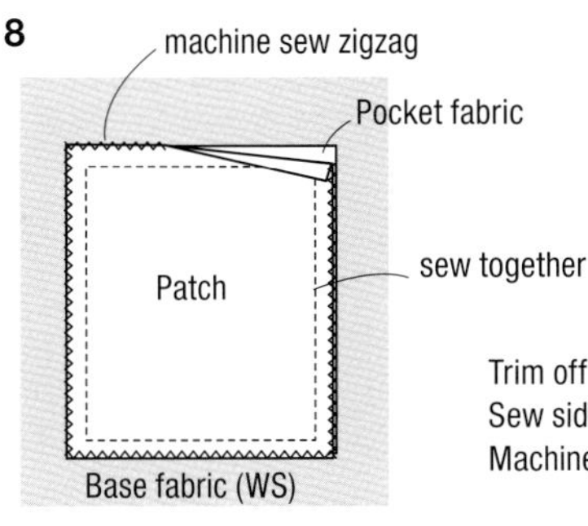

Trim off excess patch and pocket fabric.
Sew sides, except base fabric.
Machine-sew zigzag edges all the way around.

Full-Size Pattern: Hedgehog

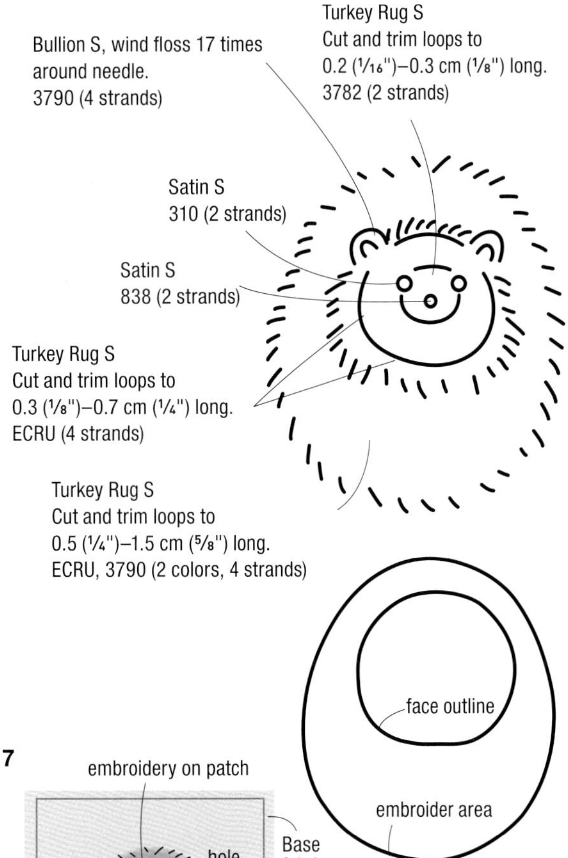

❋ Embroidering Instructions: Donkey and Fox

Donkey

1. Using long & short stitch for face, legs, and ears. Leave small unstitched areas around borders of turkey rug stitch.
2. Use turkey rug stitch for belly, forehead, and tail end. Embroider in opposite direction fur flow.
3. Make long & short stitches that overlap the turkey rug stitch base, and adjust shape.
4. Make long & short stitches to connect tail.
5. Cut and trim turkey rug stitch loops. Vary length to produce a three-dimensional effect.

Fox

1. Use long & short stitch for ears, face, legs, and body, all the while checking color shades.
2. Use straight stitch for eyes and mouth. Use satin stitch for nose.
3. Vary colors from tip of tail, using turkey rug stitches to produce gradation. Make long & short stitches that overlap base of turkey rug stitches, adjust shape.
4. Cut and trim turkey rug stitch loops. Vary length to produce fluffy tail.

Refer to pp. 63, 64.

Full-Size Pattern

Donkey

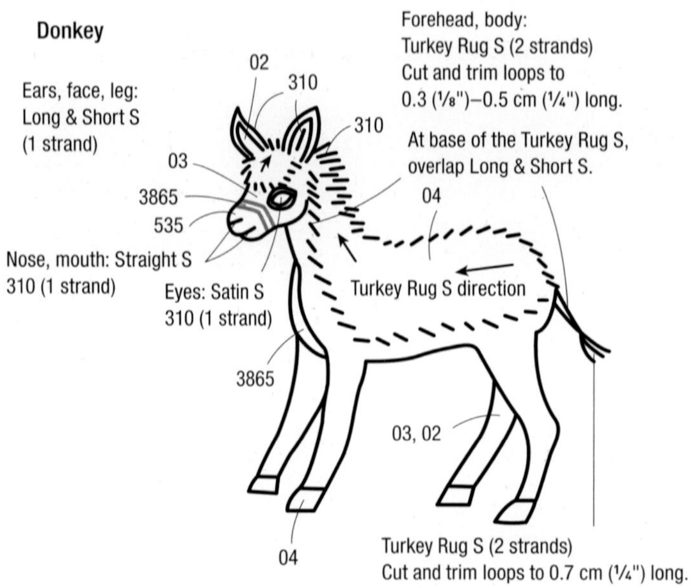

Fox

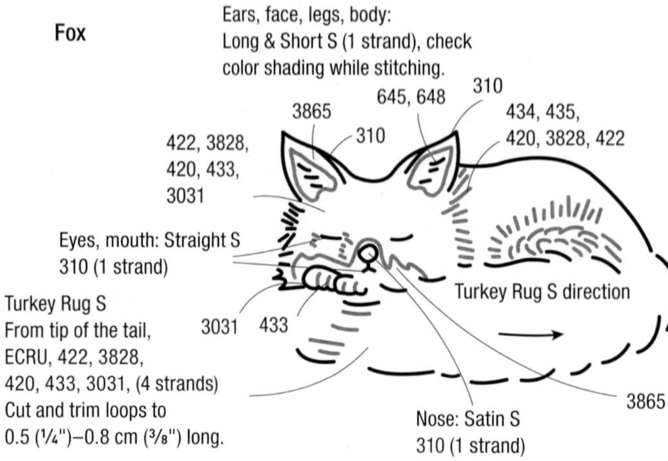

p. 27 Cats Cushion

Finished Size: 45 × 45 cm / 17¾" × 17¾"

⁂ You Will Need

Outer fabric 100 × 55 cm / 39⅜" × 21⅝"

Lining fabric 50 × 50 cm / 19¾" × 19¾"

One 45 cm / 17¾" long zipper

One cushion insert

DMC No. 25 six-stranded embroidery floss: ECRU, 02, 03, 04, 05, 07, 08, 225, 310, 317, 648, 676, 3031, 3053, 3078, 3752, 3865

⁂ Notes

- Seam allowance: 1 cm / ⅜"
- Produce a three-dimensional effect by cutting and trimming off turkey rug stitch loops to desired length.
- Feel free to use your preferred color for cat fur.

⁂ Embroidering Instructions

1. Use long & short stitch and satin stitch for ears.
2. Anywhere you don't use turkey rug stitches for the eyes, nose, legs, and tail, use long & short stitch and satin stitch.
3. Use turkey rug stitch for fur. Stitch from outside to inside along contour, keeping fur flow in mind. Also follow pattern of ears.
4. Cut and trim off turkey rug stitch loops to produce a three-dimensional effect. It's fine to mix uncut loops with cut loops.

⁂ Sewing Instructions

1. Embroider on front outer fabric. Align lining fabric on wrong side.
2. Install zipper on backside of outer fabric.
3. Put front side and backside of outer fabric together, right sides facing inward. Sew sides.
4. Machine-sew zigzag along edges.
5. Put cushion insert inside cover.

Outer Fabric Front: 1 piece
Lining Fabric: 1 piece

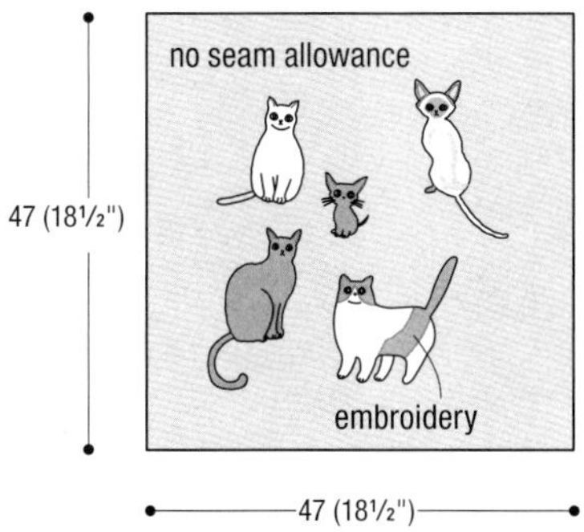

* No embroidery on backside

Outer Fabric Backside Top: 1 piece

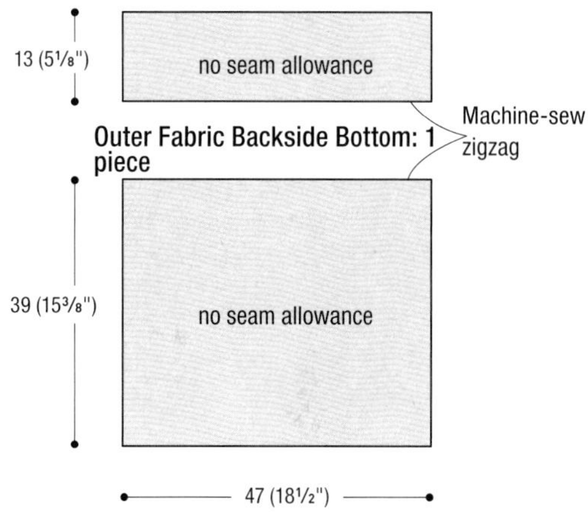

How to Sew Backside of Outer Fabric

1

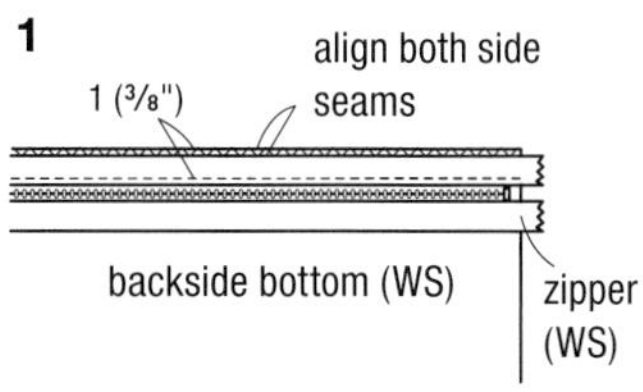

Sew zipper on backside bottom fabric.

2

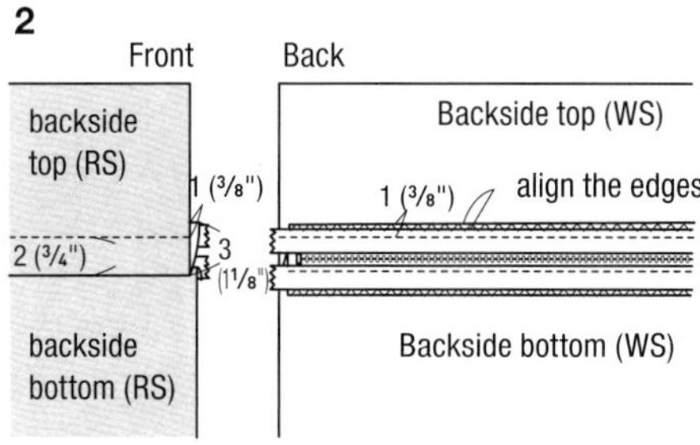

Fold bottom edge of backside top fabric down 3 cm (1⅛") and lay on zipper fabric.
With wrong side facing up, sew.

Steps

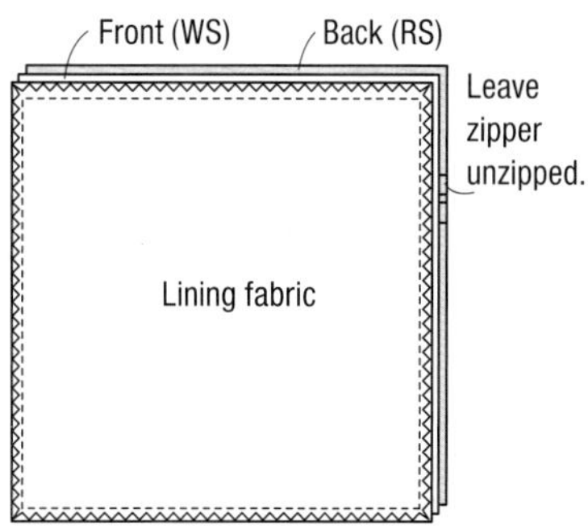

Layer front-side outer fabric and lining fabric.
With right sides together, align backside outer fabric. Sew sides.
Machine-sew zigzag along seam allowance.

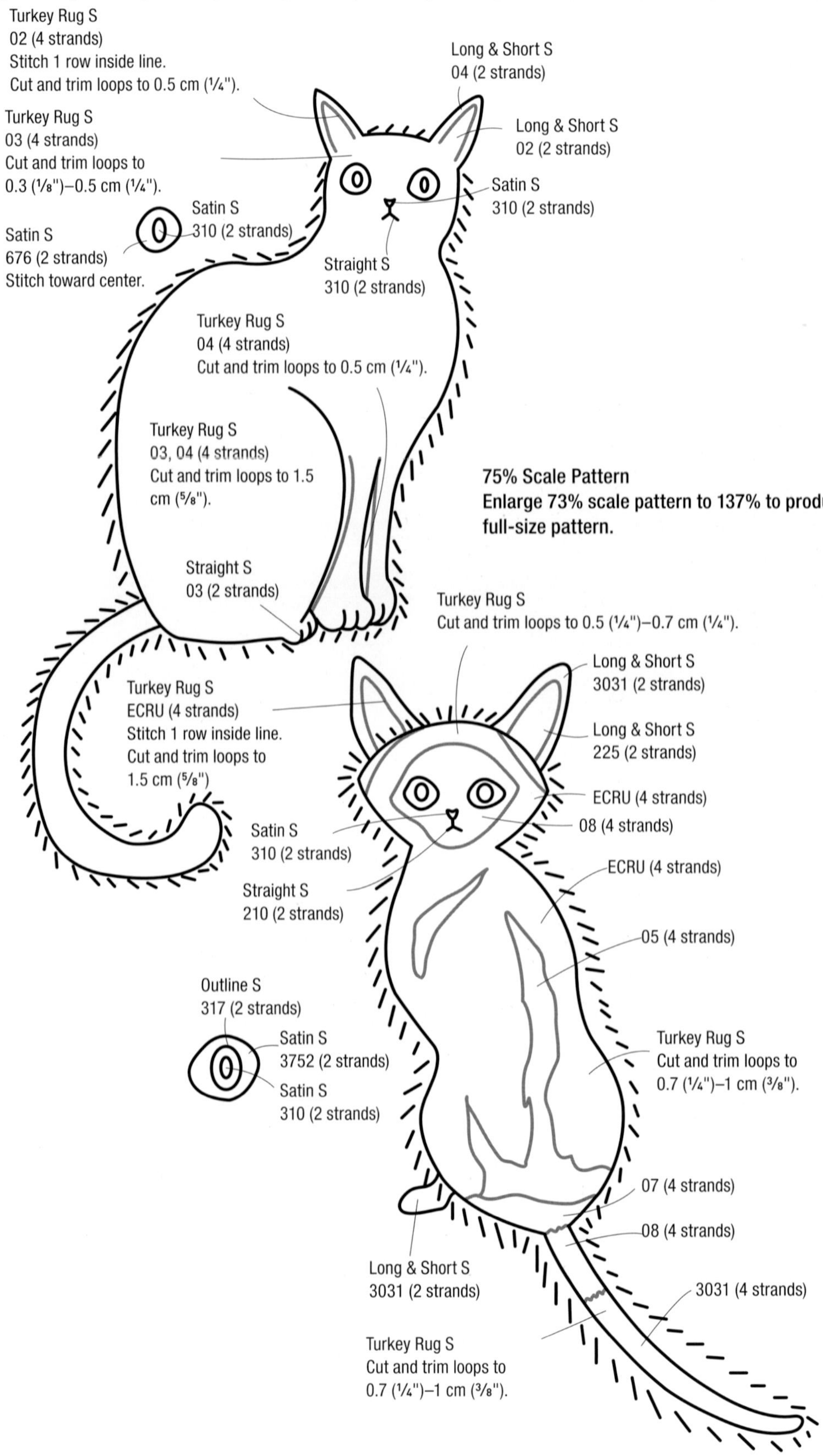

75% Scale Pattern
Enlarge 73% scale pattern to 137% to produce full-size pattern.

73% Scale Pattern
Enlarge 73% scale pattern to 137% to produce full-size pattern.

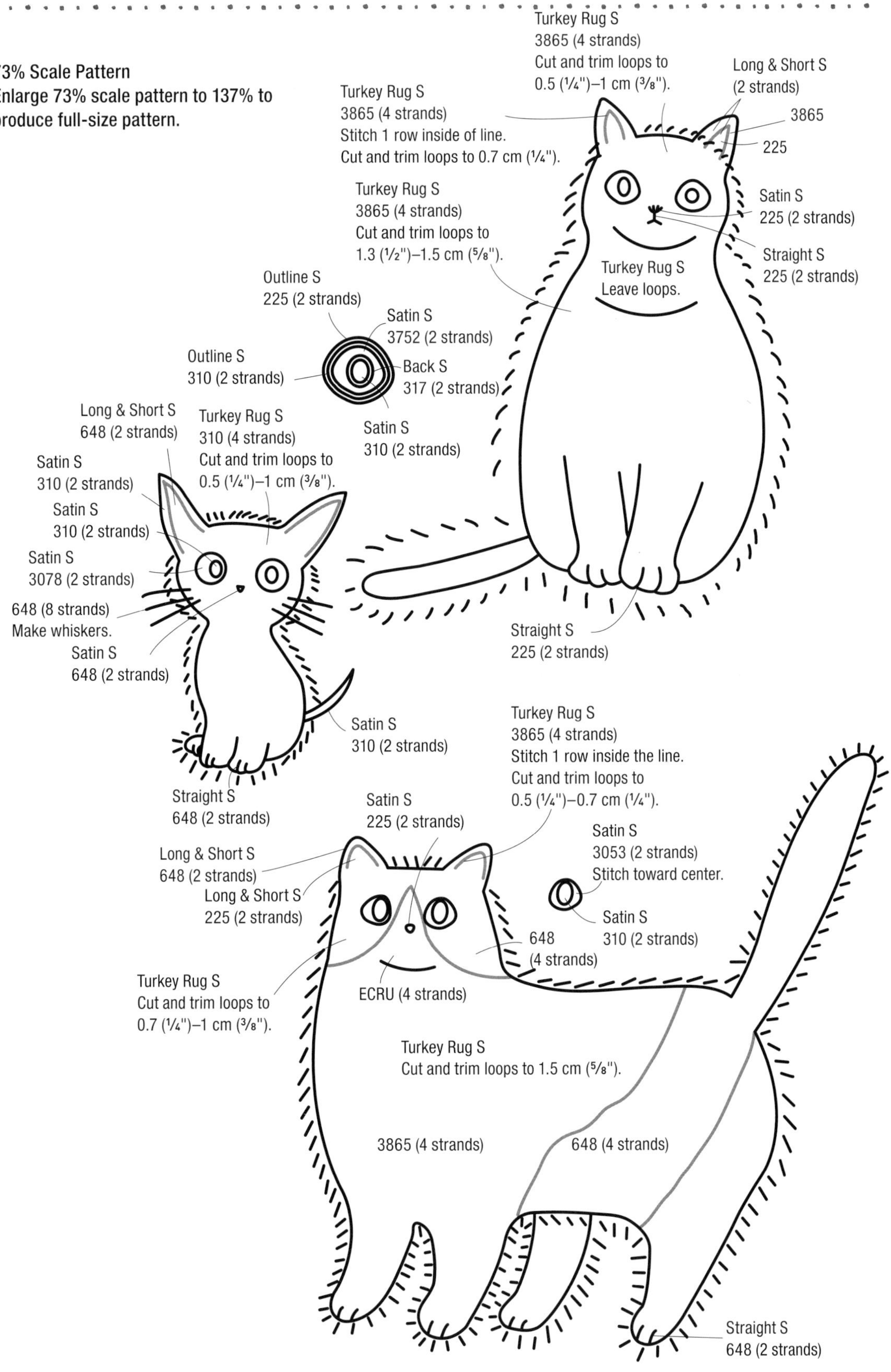

p. 29 Cat Bag

Finished Size: 39 × 48 cm / 15⅜" × 18⅞"

⋇ You Will Need

Outer fabric (including handles, outside pocket) 75 × 100 cm / 29½" × 43⅜"

Lining fabric (including outside pocket lining, inside pocket) 110 × 80 cm / 43⅜" × 30½"

One 20 cm / 7⅞" long zipper

A pair of 2 cm / ¾" diameter sew-on snap fasteners

DMC No. 25 six-stranded embroidery floss: ECRU, 225, 422, 738, 739, 761, 3828, 3865

⋇ Notes

- Add 1 cm / ⅜" seam allowance.
- Make outside pocket lining slightly smaller than outside pocket fabric.

⋇ Embroidering Instructions

1. Use long and short stitch for ears and center of face. Then, tightly cover the remaining area and adjust shape. Where necessary, combine two strands of single-color floss and two strands of different-colored floss to produce gradation. Refer to p. 63.
2. Use turkey rug stitch for the paws, changing colors in sequence. Cut and trim loops to create a round, three-dimensional effect.
3. Use outline stitch for the paws.

⋇ Sewing Instructions

1. Embroider on outer fabric. Make outside pocket and sew on outer fabric.
2. Fold outer fabric in half with right sides together. Sew both side seams and box corners.
3. Make inside pockets and sew them on lining fabric.
4. Put two pieces of lining fabric together with right sides facing in. Sew side seams, bottom, and box corners.
5. Make handles.
6. Temporarily fasten handles to outer fabric. Align lining and outer fabric, right sides together, and sew along top edge.
7. Turn right side out, close the opening for turning, and then stitch along top edge.

Outer Fabric: 1 piece

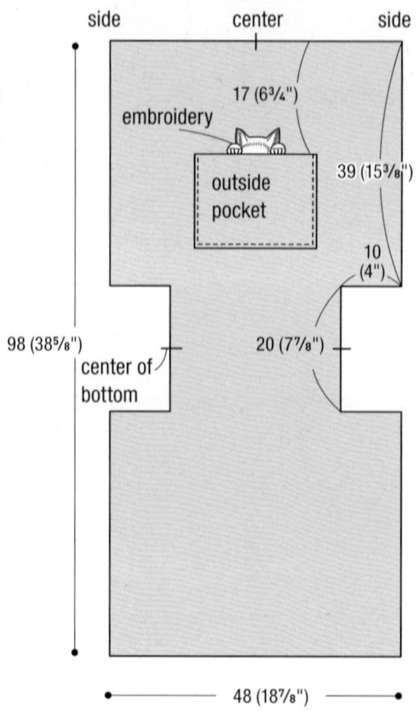

Lining-Fabric Front: 1 piece

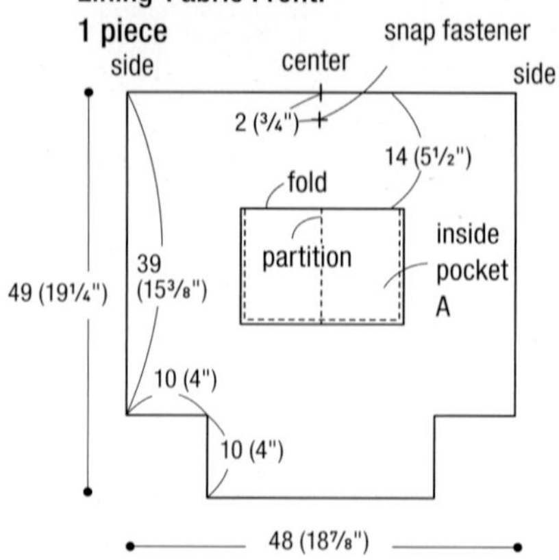

Handle: 2 pieces

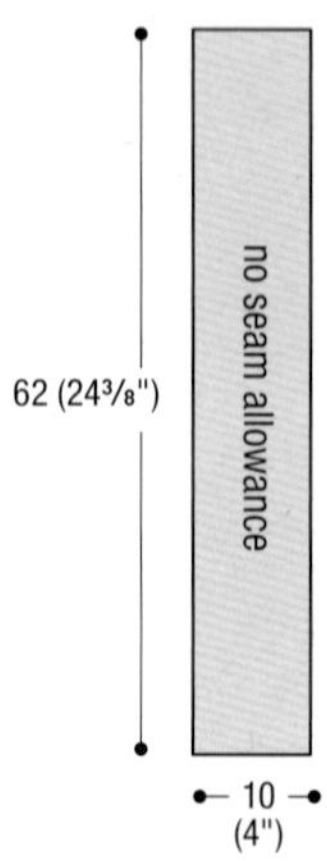

Lining-Fabric Back: 1 piece

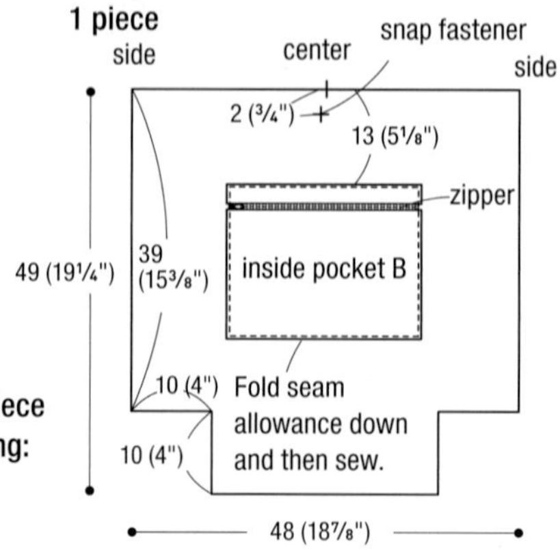

How to Make Handle

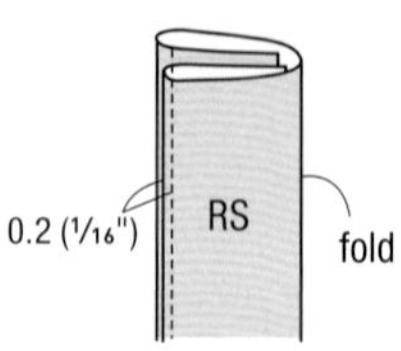

With right side facing out, fold in four and sew the side seam.

Outside Pocket: 1 piece
Outside Pocket Lining: 1 piece

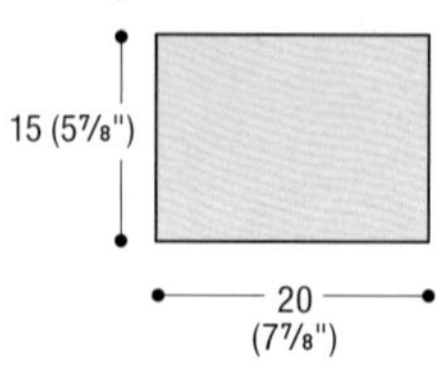

Inside Pocket A: 1 piece

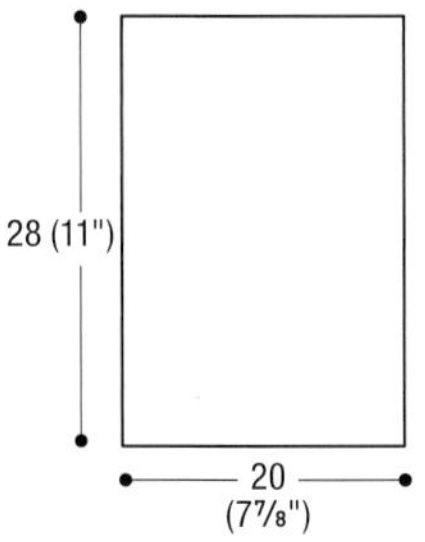

Inside Pocket B Top: 1 piece

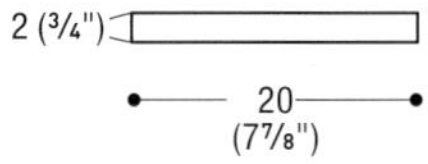

* See p. 74 for sewing instructions.

Inside Pocket B Bottom: 1 piece

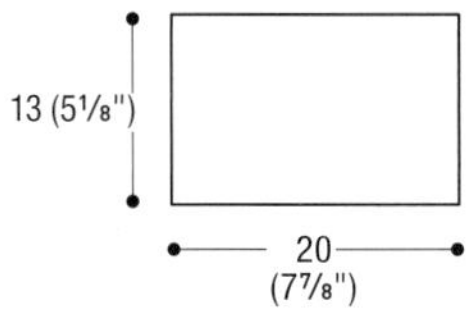

How to Sew the Lining Fabric

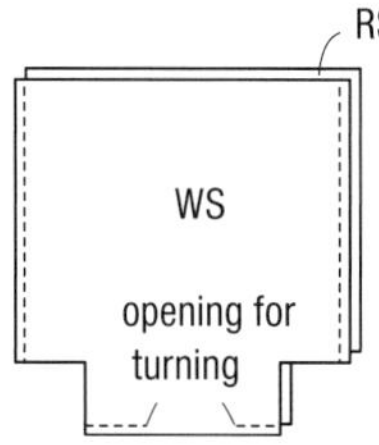

Put back and front lining fabric together, right sides in.
Sew both side seams and bottom while leaving an opening for turning.

How to Make Inside Pocket A

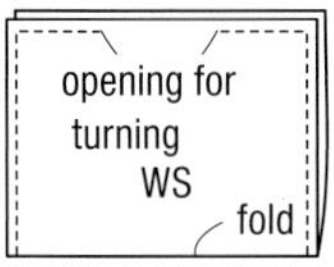

Fold in half with right sides together.
Sew sides, while leaving an opening for turning.
Turn right side out and close opening used for turning.

How to Make Outside Pocket

1

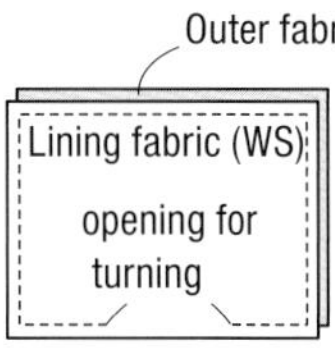

Align outer and lining fabric with right sides together.
Sew sides, but leave an opening for turning.

2

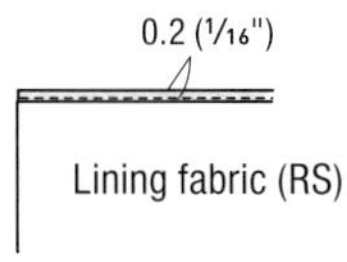

Turn right side out and close opening for turning.
Pull down top edge seam of lining and sew.

Steps

1

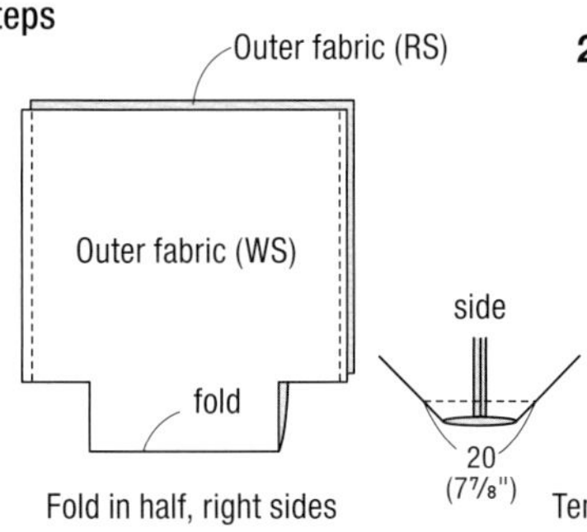

Fold in half, right sides together.
Sew both side seams and box corners.

2

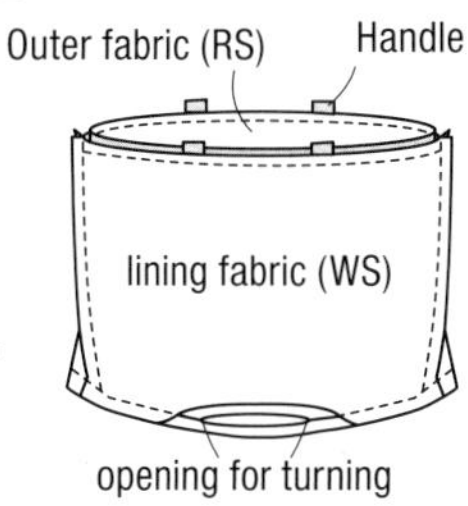

Temporarily secure handle on top edge seam allowance.
Put outer fabric inside lining, right sides together, and sew along top edge.

3

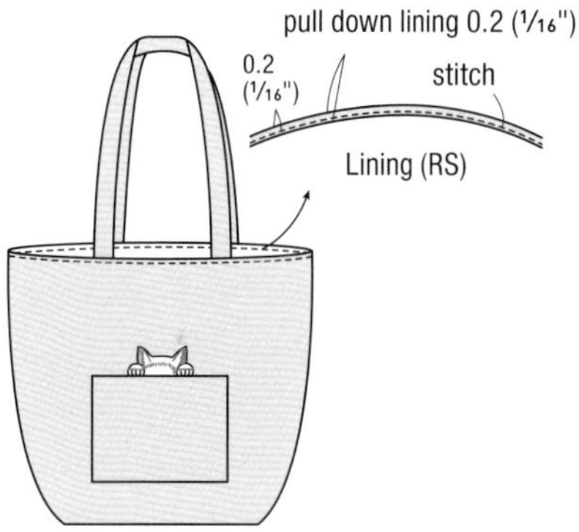

Turn right side out. Blind-stitch to close opening for turning.
Stitch along top edge and attach snap fastener.

Full-Size Pattern

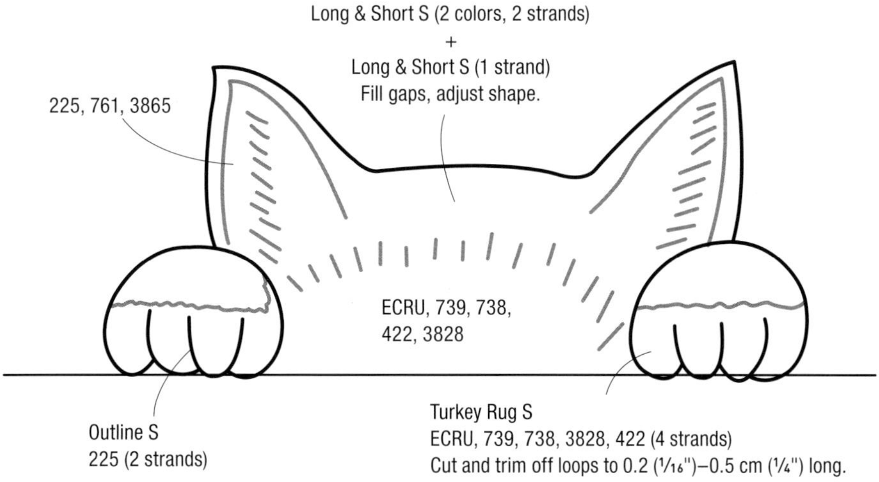

p. 30 Squirrel Blanket

Finished Size: 150 × 93 cm / 59" × 36⅝"

⋇ You Will Need

Wool outer fabric 100 × 160 cm / 39⅜" × 63"

DMC No. 25 six-stranded Embroidery Floss: 310, 433, 434, 838, 839, 840, 841, 842, 3862, 3866

⋇ Note

- Add 3 cm / 1⅛" seam allowance.

⋇ Embroidering Instructions

1. Use long and short stitch for body, head, and legs while checking shading. Then, stitch further to fill. Where necessary, combine two strands of single-color floss and two strands of different-colored floss to produce gradation.
2. Use turkey knot stitch for ears while keeping fur flow in mind. Overlap and nestle long & short stitch at base of turkey knot stitches.
3. Use turkey rug stitch to work tail, starting from its end, changing colors in sequence. Overlap and nestle long & short stitches at base of turkey rug stitches.
   Refer to pp. 63, 64.

⋇ Sewing Instructions

1. Embroider the design.
2. Fold edges in three and sew.

Blanket: 1 piece

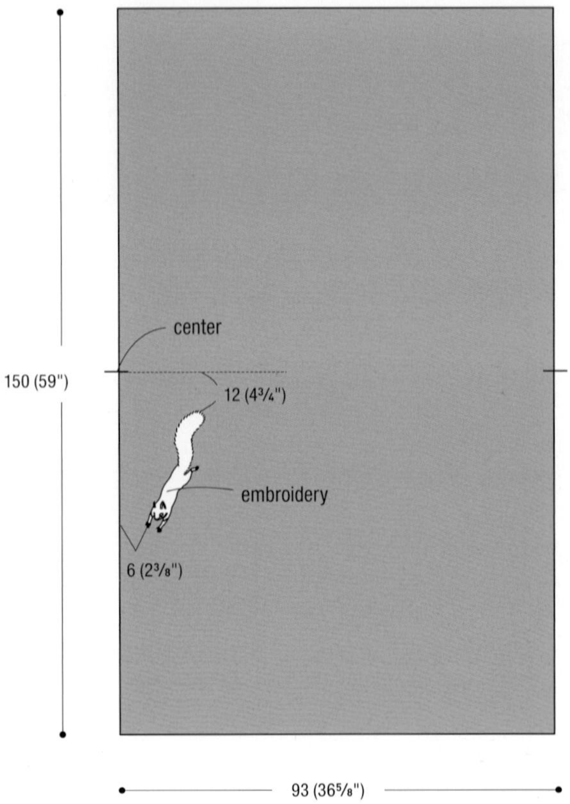

Steps

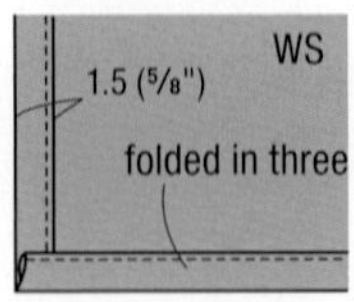

Fold in three and sew sides.

80% Scale Pattern

Enlarge the 80% scale pattern to 125% to produce the full-size pattern.

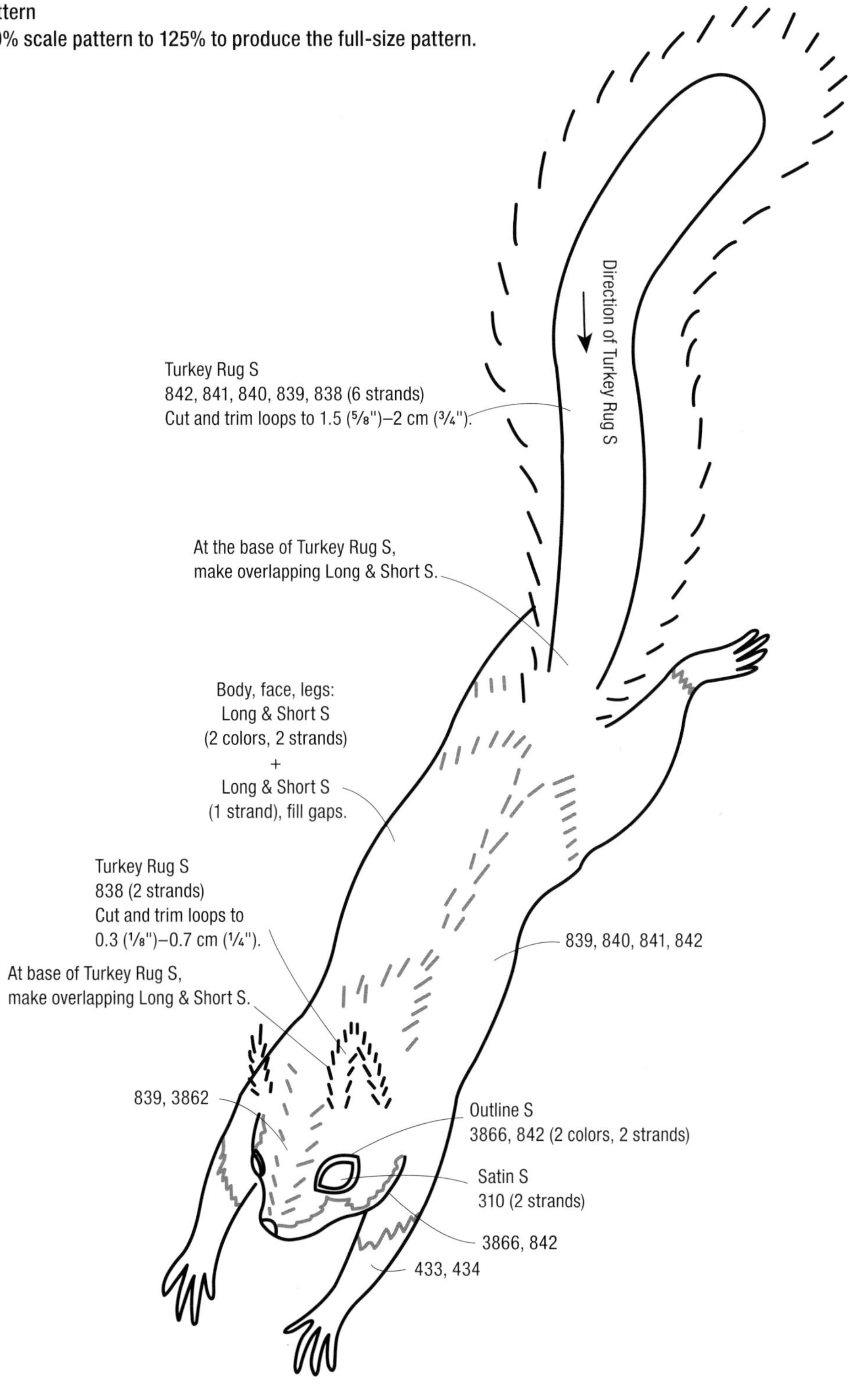

p. 32 Swallow

80% Scale Pattern. Enlarge 80% scale pattern to 125% to produce full-size pattern.

⌘ Embroidering Instructions

1. Embroider the wings. Fill area with long & short stitch and outline with satin stitch.
2. Use satin stitch for beak and eye.
3. Embroider body. Work long and short stitches, using three different colors of floss. Keep feather flow in mind and fill in spaces between stitches further. Make the feathers look neat. Where necessary, combine two strands of single-color floss and two strands of different-colored floss to produce gradation.

Refer to p. 63.

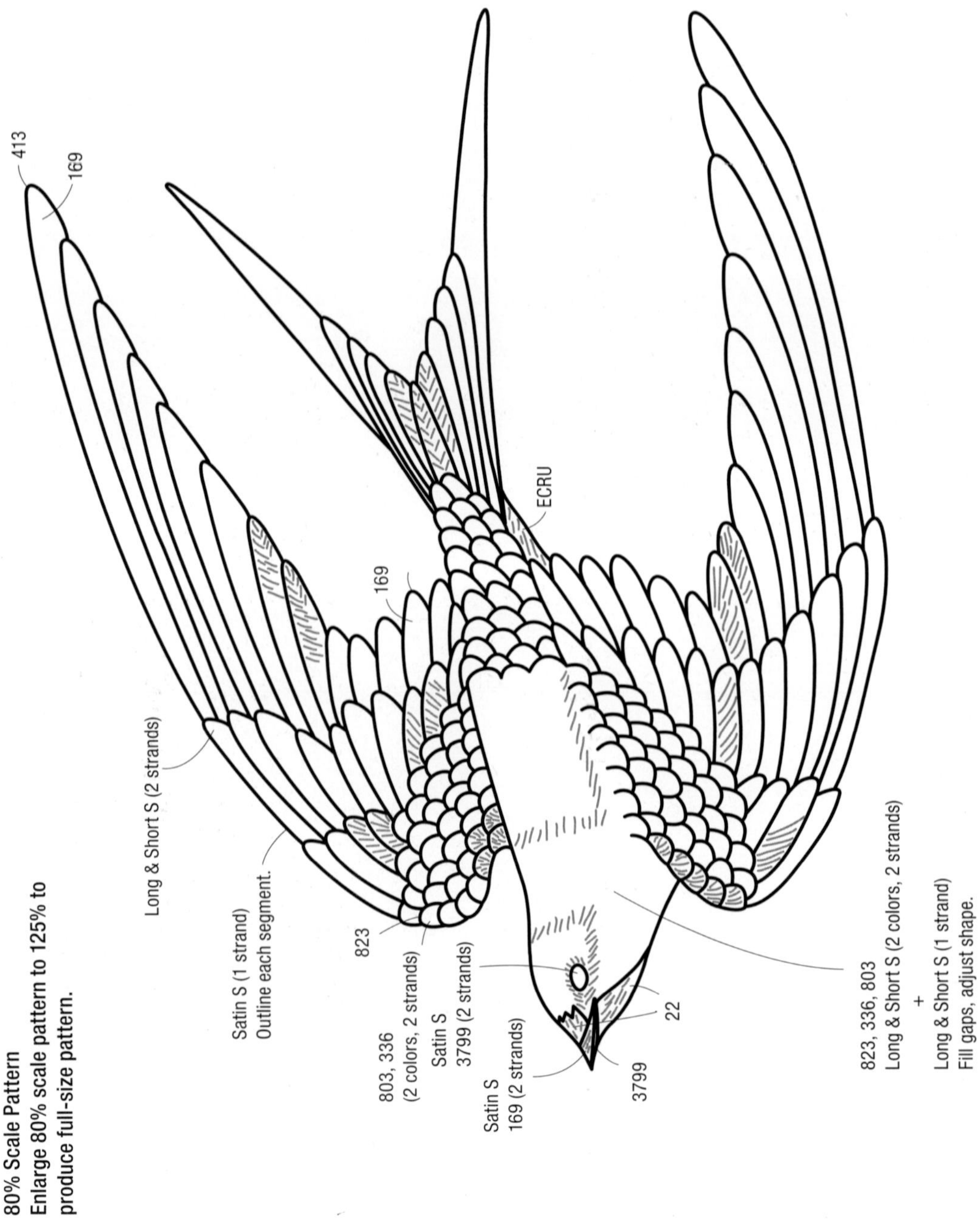

p. 33 Wing

Full-Size Pattern

⋇ Embroidering Instructions

1. Use long & short stitches to fill area.
2. Fill area further using long & short stitches in spaces between the other stitches.

Refer to p. 63.

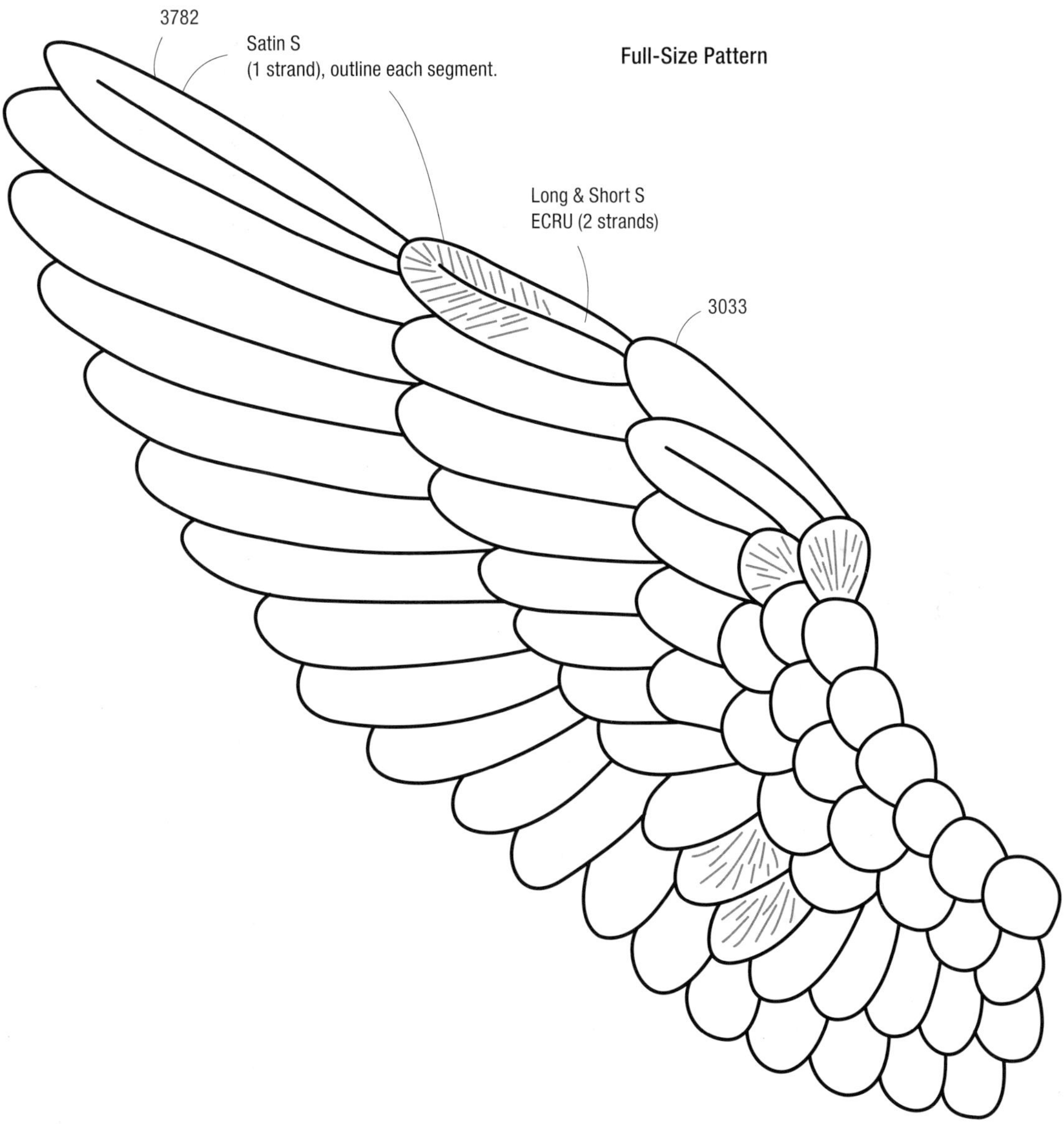

p. 34 Swallow Bag

Finished Size: 32 × 23 cm / 12⅝" × 9"

⁂ You Will Need

Outer fabric (includes handles) 70 × 65 cm / 27½" × 25⅝"

Lining fabric (includes inside pocket) 45 × 70 cm / 15¾" × 27½"

DMC No. 25 six-stranded embroidery floss: ECRU

⁂ Note

- Add 1 cm / ⅜" seam allowance.

⁂ Embroidering Instructions

1. Use long & short stitch to fill area.
2. Fill area further using long & short stitch in spaces between the other stitches.

⁂ Sewing Instructions

1. Embroider on outer fabric.
2. Sew backside and front side of outer fabric, with right sides together.
3. Make inside pocket and sew it on lining fabric.
4. Fold lining fabric in half, with right sides together, and sew.
5. Make handles.
6. Temporarily fasten handles to outer fabric. Align lining and outer fabric, right sides together, and sew along top edge.
7. Turn right side out and close opening for turning. Stitch along top edge.

Outer Fabric Front: 1 piece

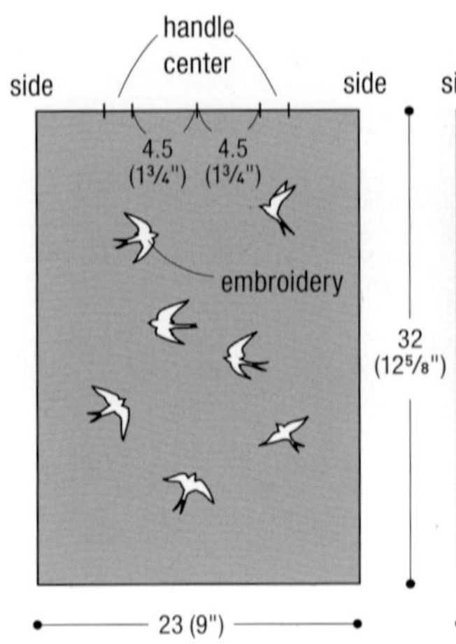

Outer Fabric Back: 1 piece

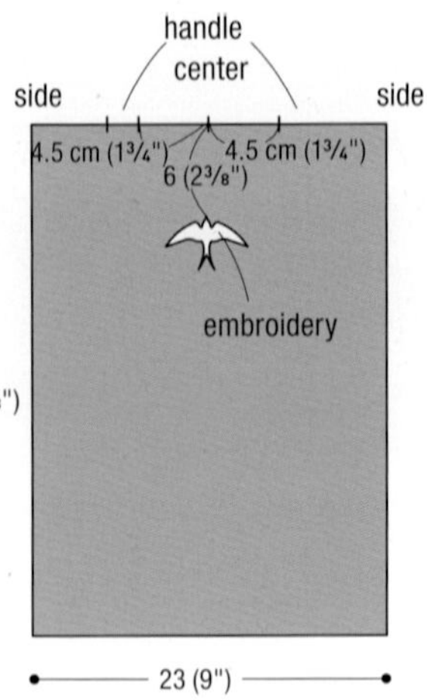

Lining Fabric: 1 piece

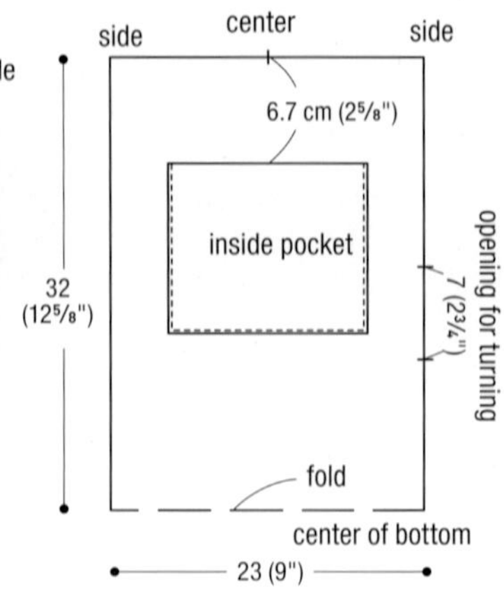

Handle: 2 pieces

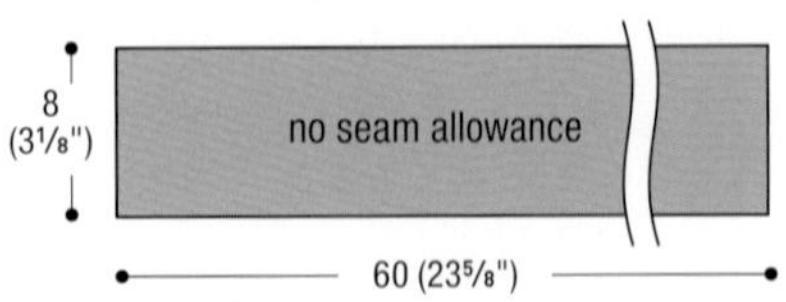

How to Sew Handles

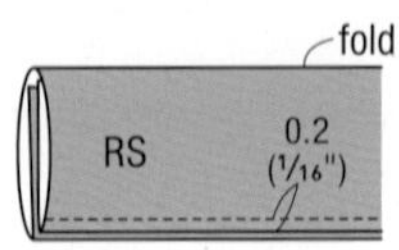

Right side facing out, fold in four then sew along edge.

Inside Pocket: 2 pieces

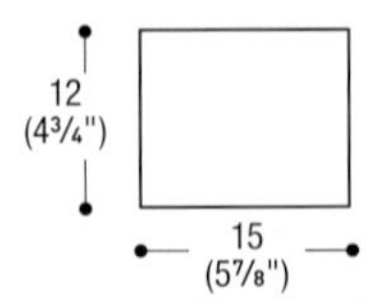

How to Sew Inside Pocket

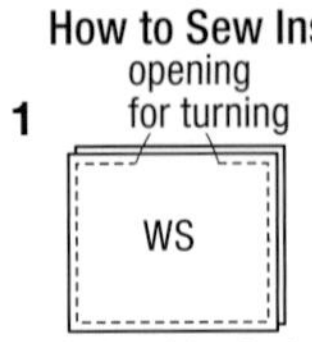

Right sides facing together, sew around edges while leaving an opening for turning.

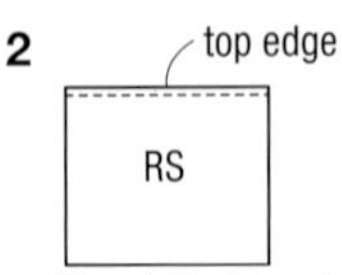

Turn right side out. Tuck in seam allowance on the opening and sew.

Steps

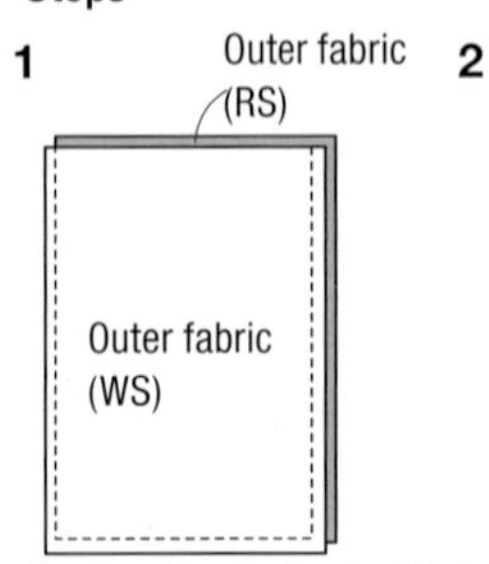

Align front and back of outer fabric with right sides together.
Sew both side seams and bottom.
Fold lining fabric in half with right sides together.
Sew both side seams, leave an opening for turning.

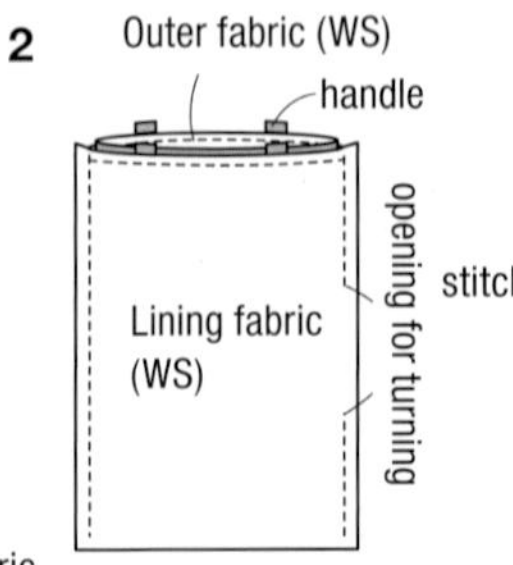

Temporarily secure handles on seam allowance along top edge.
Put outer fabric inside lining fabric, with right sides together, and sew along top edge.

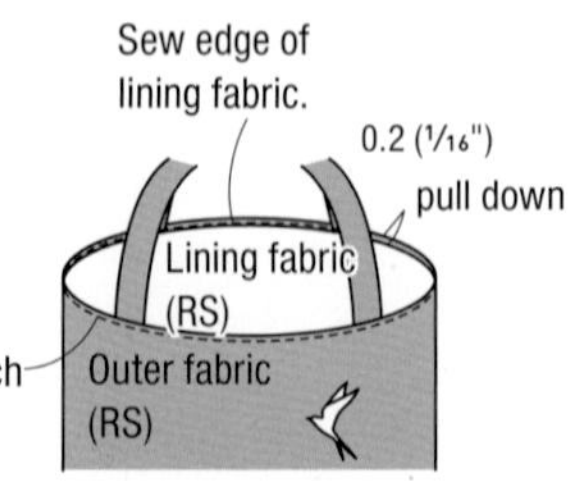

Turn right side out, blind-stitch opening for turning to close.
Stitch along top edge.

Full-Size Pattern

p. 40 Minerals

Full-Size Pattern

⋇ Embroidering Instructions

- Embroider, as envisioned, using long & short stitch, outline stitch, etc. Where necessary, combine two (or four) strands of single-color floss and two (or four) strands of different-colored floss to gradate. Refer to pp. 62, 63.
- Use couching stitch for mineral names.

Full-Size Pattern

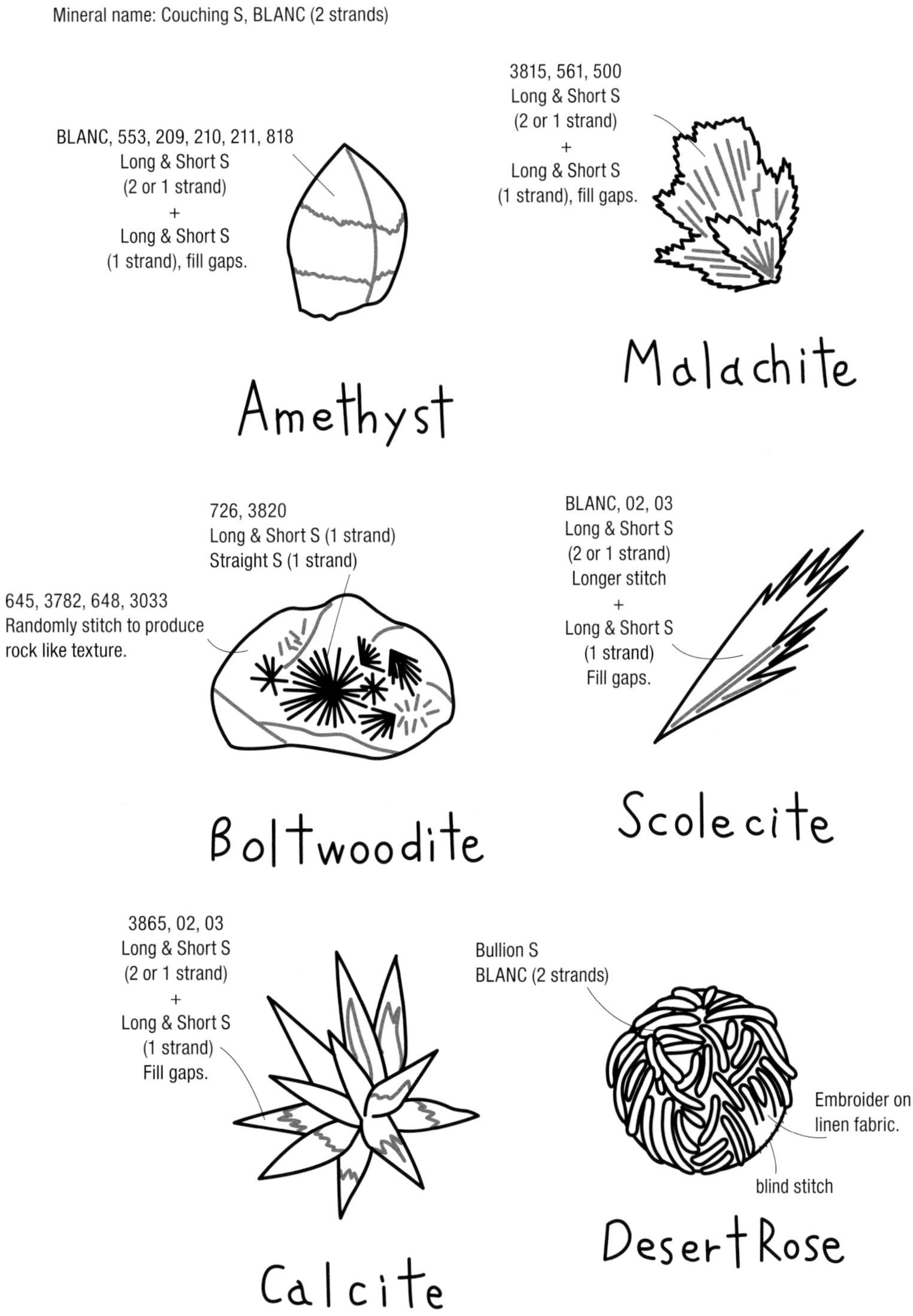

p. 41 Crystal Bookmark

Finished Size: 10 × 5.5 cm / 4" × 2⅛"

⁂ You Will Need

Outer fabric (include backside fabric) 15 × 15 cm / 5⅞" × 5⅞"

1.1 cm / ½" wide ribbon 30 cm / 11¾" long

DMC six-stranded embroidery floss: A: 151, 645, 3354, 3733

B: 210, 340, 341, 598, 645, 747, 964

⁂ Note

- Feel free to embroider any crystal from pp. 100, 101.

⁂ Embroidering Instructions

- Use long & short stitch for the crystal. Work further to tightly cover area; fill spaces between stitches. Where necessary, combine two strands of single-color floss and two strands of different-colored floss to gradate. Refer to pp. 62, 63.
- Use couching stitch for all letters.

⁂ Sewing Instructions

1. Embroider the design.
2. Sandwich ribbon between front side and backside of outer fabric. Sew sides.

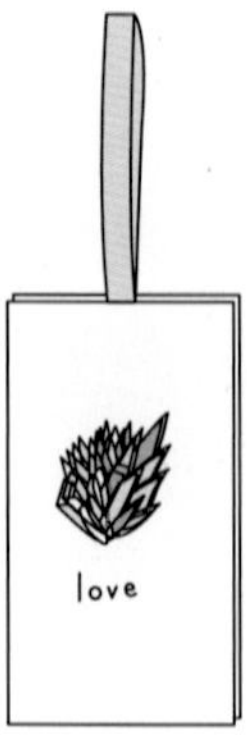

A Front Side: 1 piece

A Front Side: 1 piece

A · B Common
Backside: 1 piece

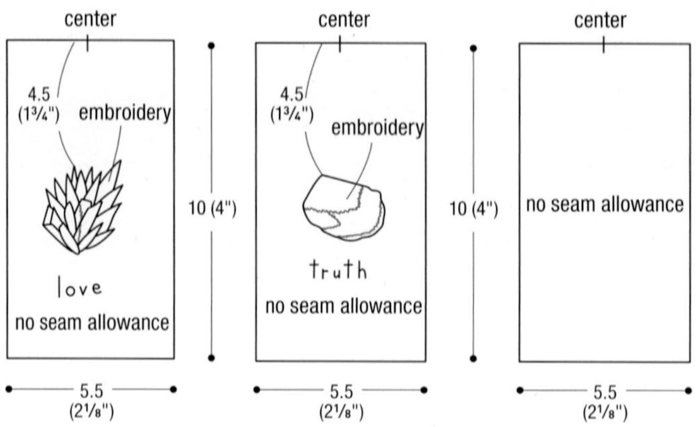

Full-Size Pattern

151, 3354, 3733
Long & Short S (2 strands)
+
Long & Short S
(1 strand)
Fill gaps.

love

Couching S
645 (2 strands)

598, 964, 747, 341, 340, 210
Long & Short S (2 strands)
+
Long & Short S
(1 strand)
Fill gaps.

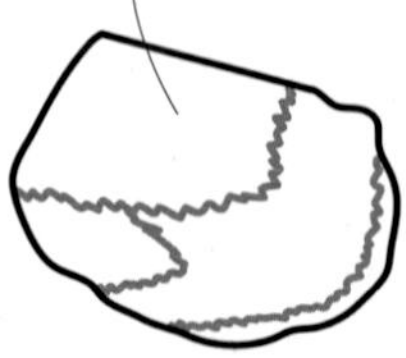

truth

Couching S
645 (2 strands)

Steps

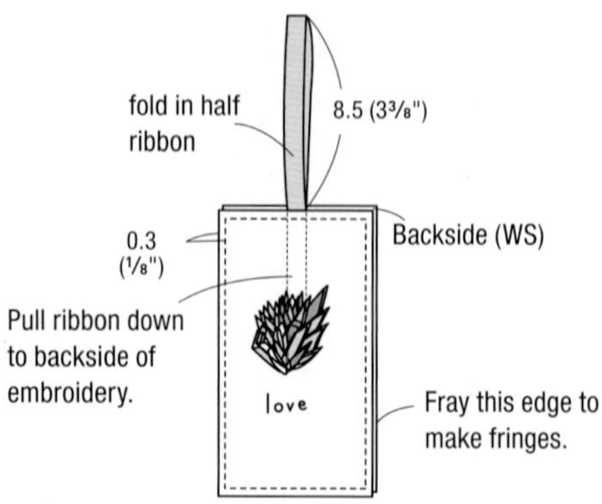

Align front side and backside, with right side out, insert ribbon, and sew sides.

p. 42 Mountain and Sea Motifs in a Frame

Finished Size—A: 9.5 × 14 cm / 3¾" × 5½" (image size), B: 8 × 11.8 cm / 3⅛" × 4⅝" (image size), C: 19 × 19 cm / 7½" × 7½" (image size)

✻ You Will Need

A: Fabric 30 × 25 cm / 11¾" × 9⅞"

Frame 9.5 × 14 cm / 3¾" × 5½" (image size)

DMC No. 25 six-stranded embroidery floss: ECRU, 07, 08, 642, 646, 647, 648, 3022, 3023, 3033, 3782, 3790, 3862, 3863

B: Fabric 25 × 25 cm / 9⅞" × 9⅞"

Frame 8 × 11.8 cm / 3⅛" × 4⅝" (image size)

DMC No. 25 six-stranded embroidery floss: 08, 838, 839, 3032, 3782, 3826, 3863

C: Fabric 40 × 40 cm / 15¾" × 15¾"

Frame 19 × 19 cm / 7½" × 7½" (image size)

DMC No. 25 six-stranded embroidery floss: BLANC, 211, 676, 3078, 3782

✻ Note

- Use your preferred frame.

✻ Embroider Instructions

- For A: Use long & short stitch for leaves and wings. Stitch further to cover area, filling in spaces between the stitches. Where necessary, combine two strands of single-color floss and two strands of different-colored floss to gradate. Refer to p. 63.
- Refer to figure below for honeycomb couching stitch.
- For leaves on B,

1 Use outline stitch to work leaf center and veins.
2 Use long & short stitch to fill area. Stitch further to tightly fill the area and adjust leaf shape.
3 Use lace-filling stitch for withered areas on the leaf.

- Satin stitch on coral in C starts at the thick end and becomes an outline stitch as it moves to the thin end. Use outline stitch as you move to the narrow end.

✻ Sewing Instructions

1. Embroider the design.
2. Wrap backing board and install frame.

A

B

C

A Fabric: 1 piece

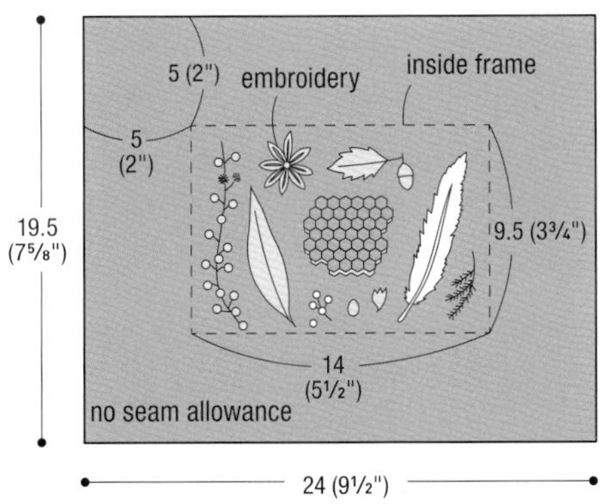

B Fabric: 1 piece

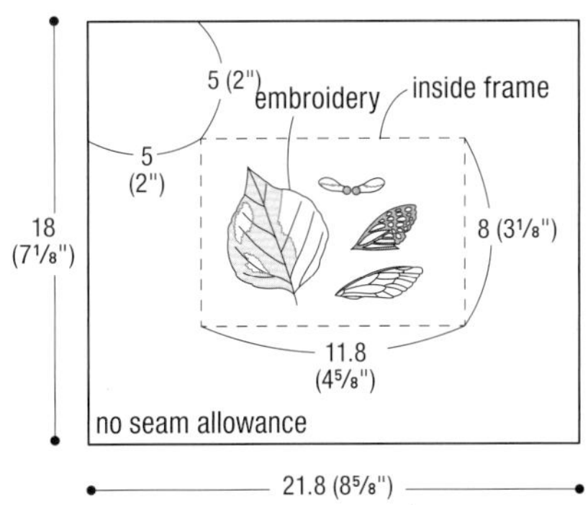

C Fabric: 1 piece

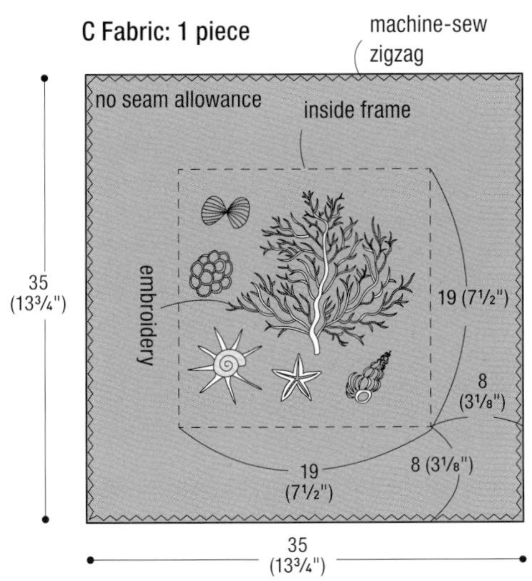

Steps

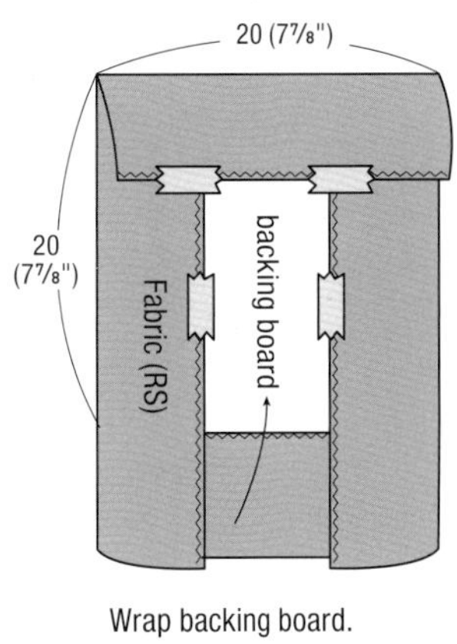

Wrap backing board. Secure with tape. Mount on frame.

Full-Size Pattern

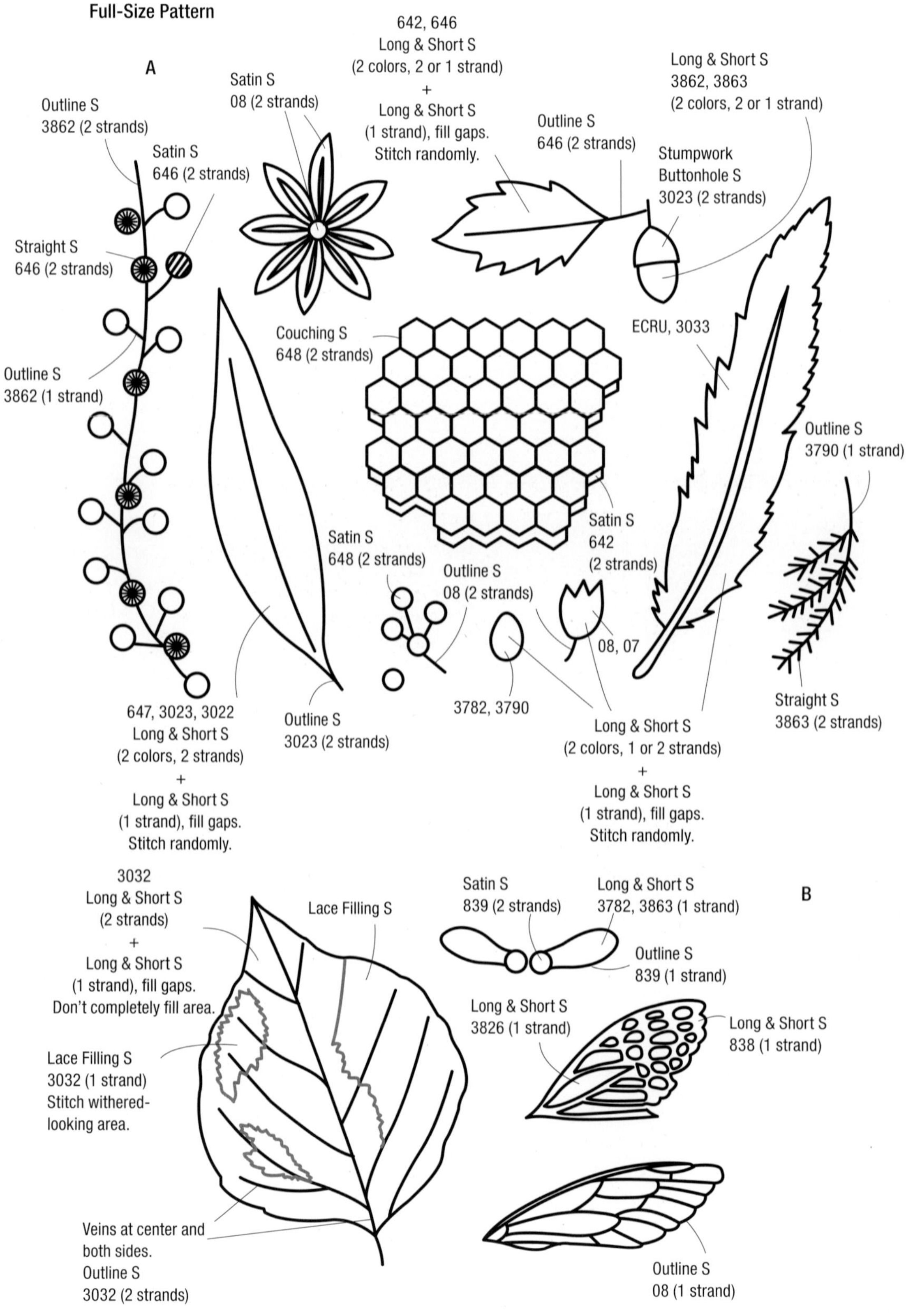

Full-Size Pattern

C

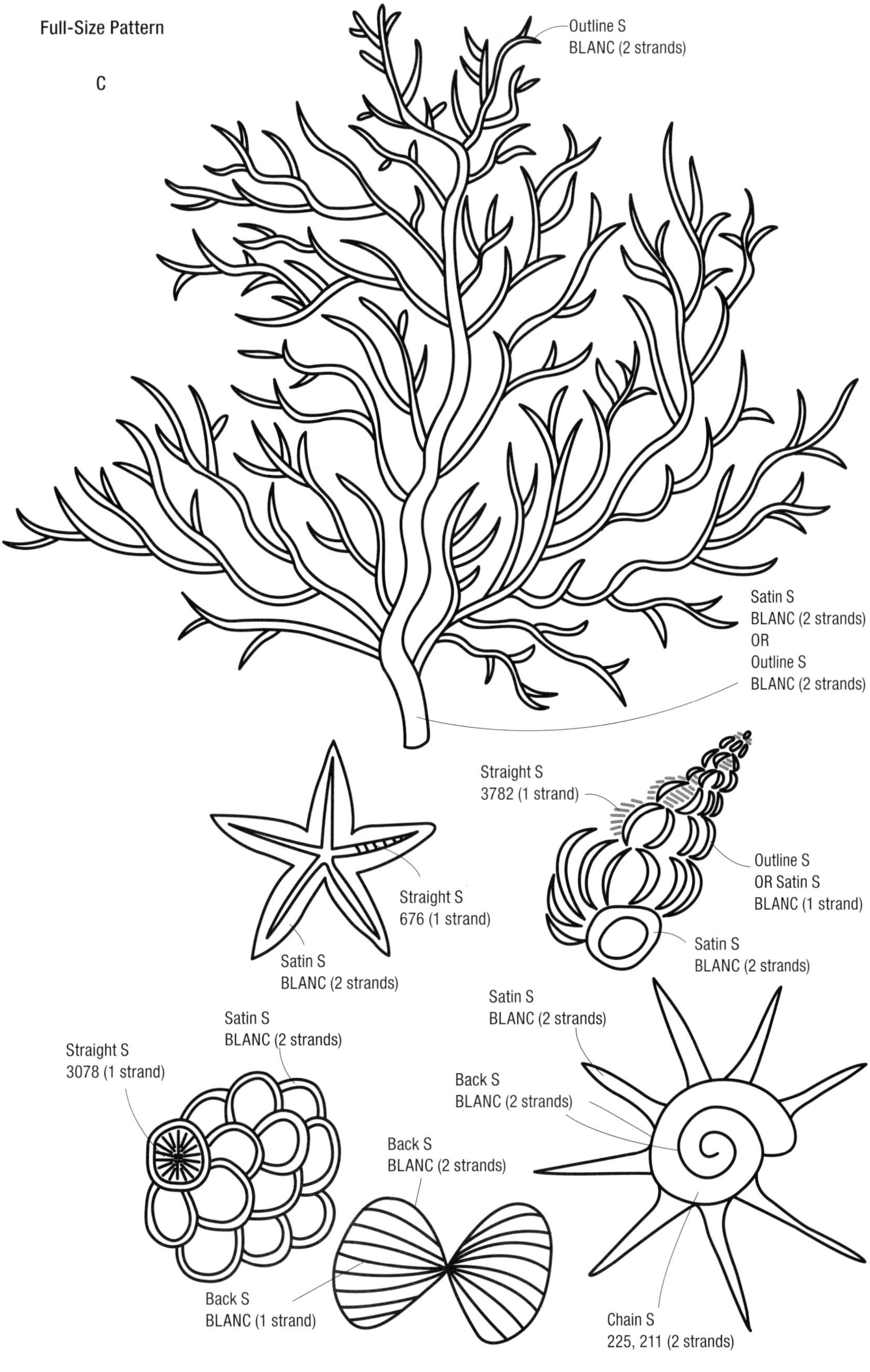

p. 36 Galaxy Swallow

Full-Size Pattern

※ Embroidering Instructions

1. Use long & short stitch for the swallow. Feel free to choose any swallow you wish from p. 98.
2. Use straight stitch for the Milky Way. Feel free to use other types of stitch as well.

Full-Size Pattern

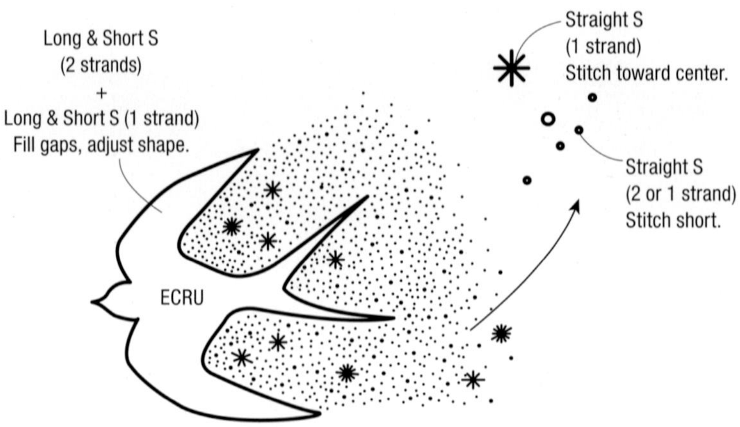

p. 47 Lemon Bag

Finished Size: 14 × 11 cm / 5½" × 4⅜"

⋇ You Will Need

Organza 15 × 35 cm / 5⅞" × 13¾"

2.5 cm / 1" wide ribbon, 100 cm / 39⅜"

DMC No. 25 six-stranded embroidery floss: 307, 3078, 3865

⋇ Note

- Work lemon as desired. The work on p. 46 embroidered multiple lemon slices on organza as desired.

⋇ Embroidering Instructions

1. Use satin stitch, at an angle, for the yellow rind.
2. Use long & short stitch, all in a uniform direction, to work white pith.
3. Use backstitch for membrane walls. Last, bind floss at center.
4. Use lace-filling stitch for membrane. Also, refer to p. 60.

⋇ Sewing Instructions

1. Embroider design on organza.
2. Sew top and bottom edges and fold fabric in half. Cover each side with ribbon.

Organza: 1 piece

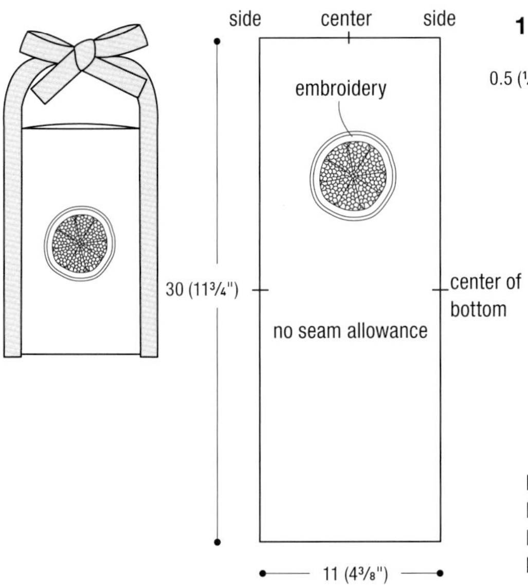

Steps

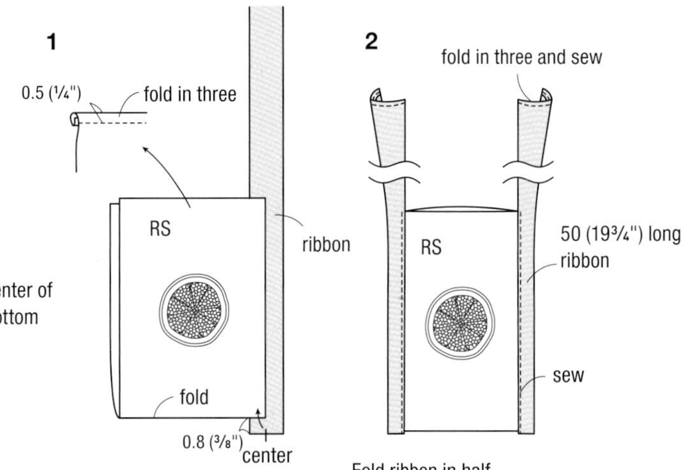

Fold top and bottom edge in three. Fold organza in half, right side out. Lay ribbon on side and wrap bottom corner.

Fold ribbon in half. Fold top edge of ribbon in three and sew.

Full-Size Pattern

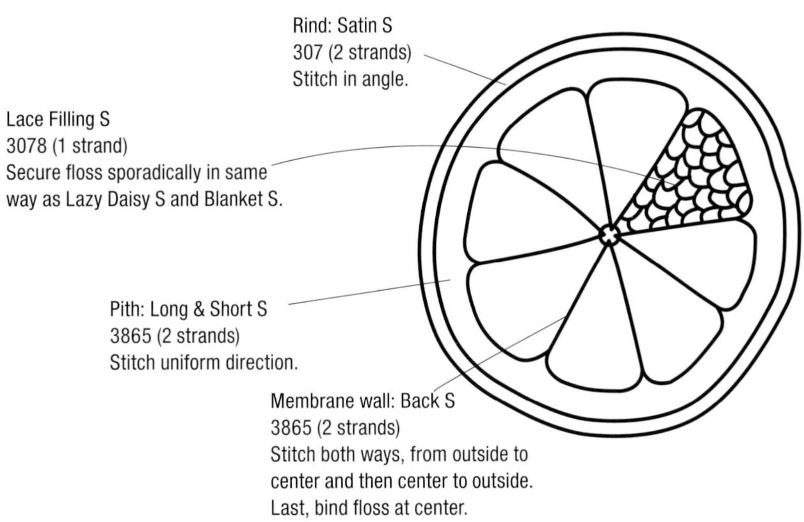

p. 48 Beach

80% Scale Pattern. Enlarge 80% scale pattern to 125% to produce full-size pattern.

❋ Embroidering Instructions

- Embroider, as desired, using long & short stitches, satin stitches, outline stitches, straight stitches, chain stitches, etc.
- Embroidering Floss: Skin color—ECRU, 422, 739 / Hair color—08, 676, 3826 / use desired color or leftover floss for clothes.
- Try this design on various items, such as a shirt or bag.

80% Scale Pattern.
Enlarge 80% scale pattern to 125% to produce full-size pattern.

Skin color:
ECRU, 422, 739

Hair color:
08, 676, 3826

Clothes:
Combine color as desired.

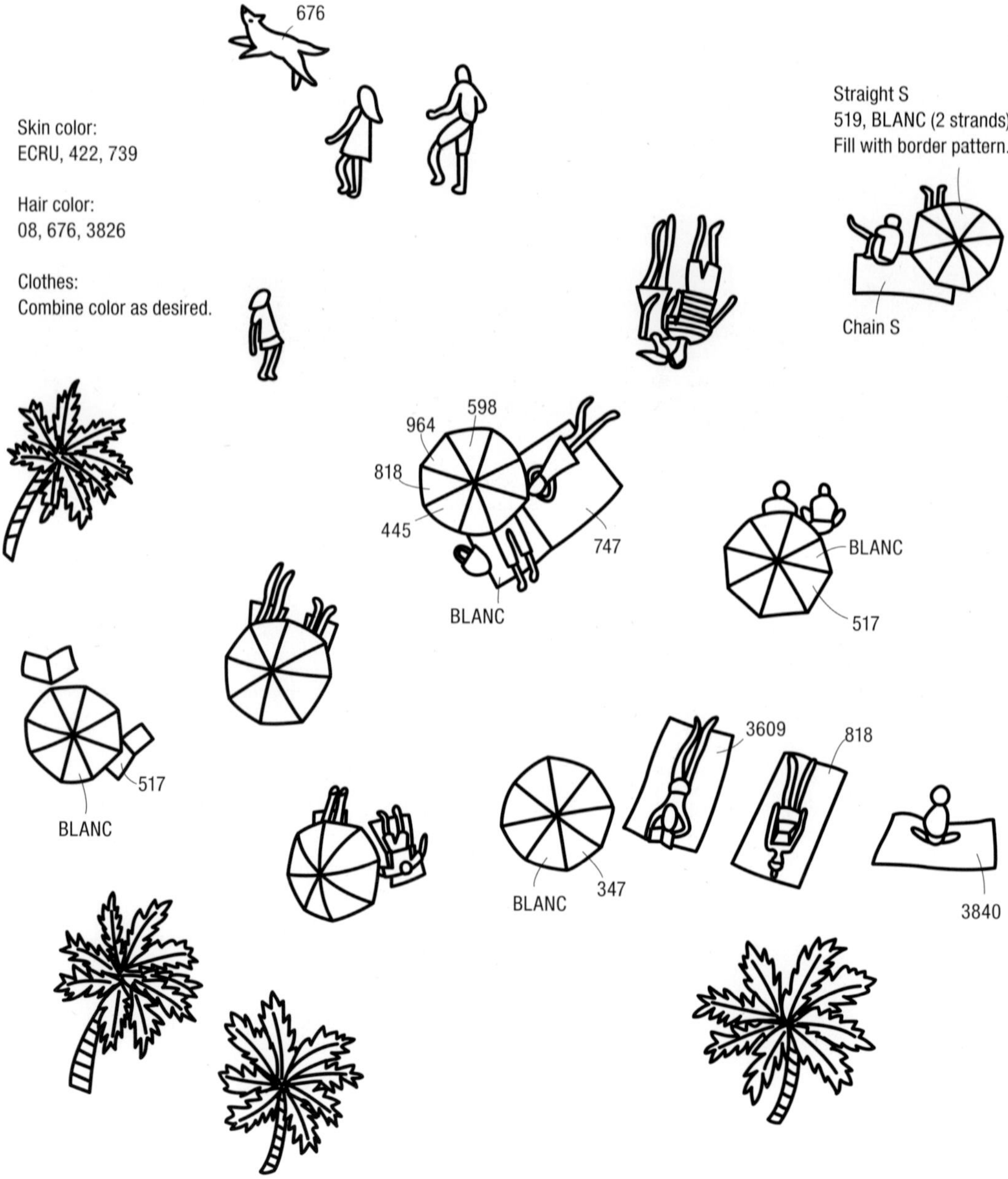

Embroidery Position

Adapt pattern and embroider on any item you desire.

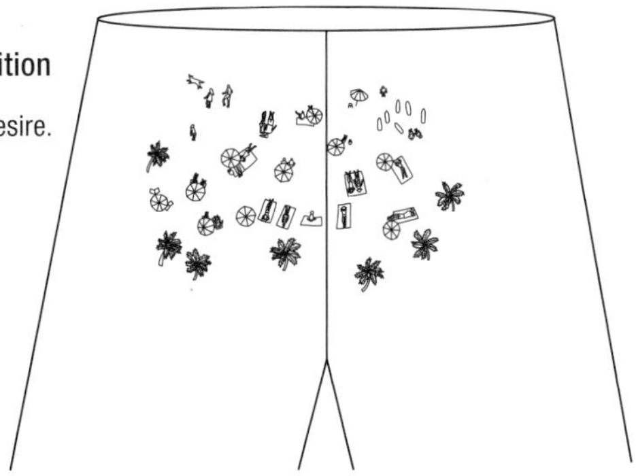

80% Scale Pattern.
Enlarge 80% scale pattern to 125% to produce full-size pattern.

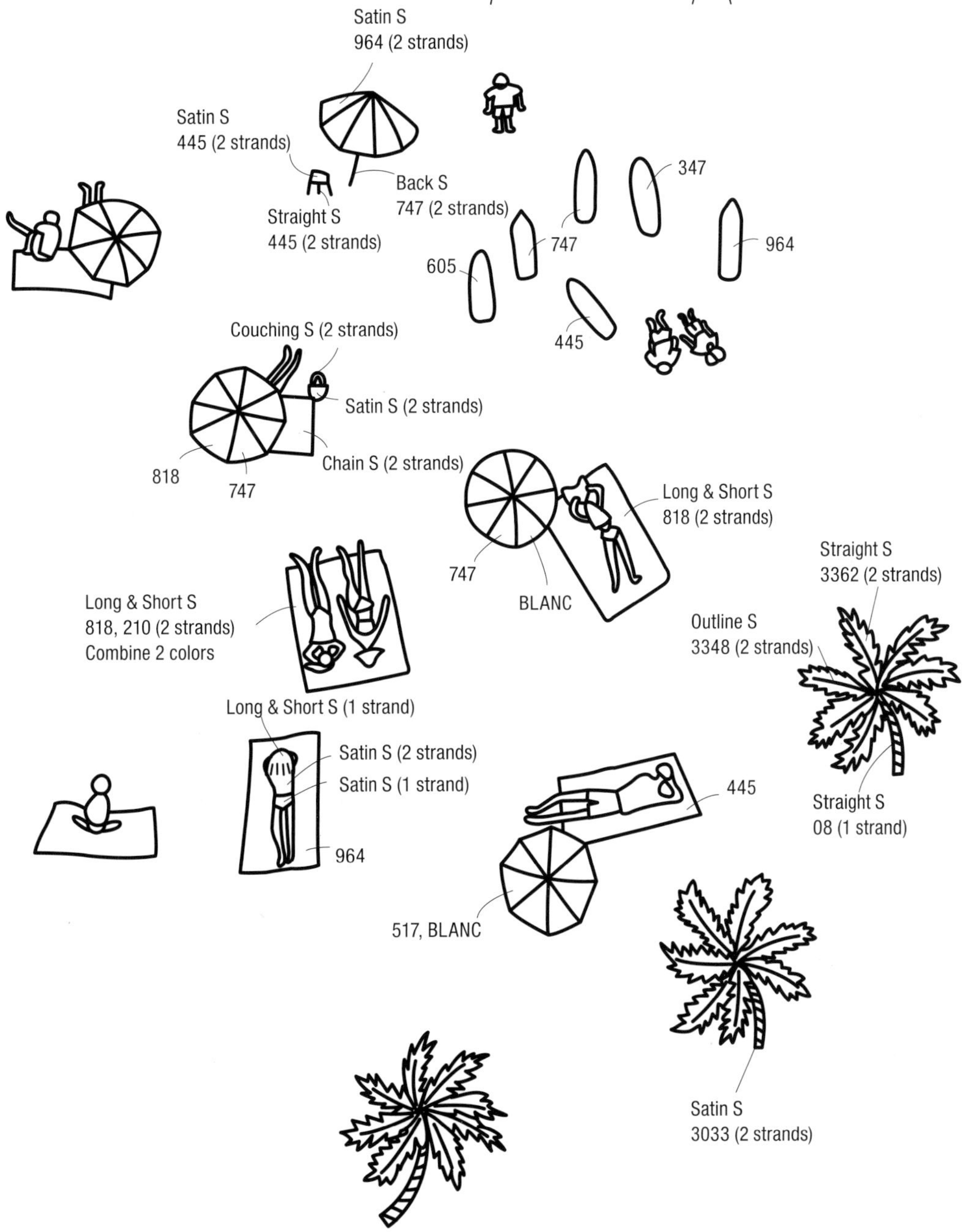

p. 51 Skiing

73% Scale Pattern. Enlarge 73% scale pattern to 137% to produce full-size pattern.

⁂ Embroidering Instructions

- Stitch mountains only where necessary, while still taking advantage of fabric color. Also, where necessary, combine two strands of single-color floss and two strands of different-colored floss to gradate.
- Freely stitch using long & short stitch, satin stitch, outline stitch, straight stitch, etc.
- Use desired color or leftover floss for clothes.
- Try this design on various items, such as a shirt or bag.

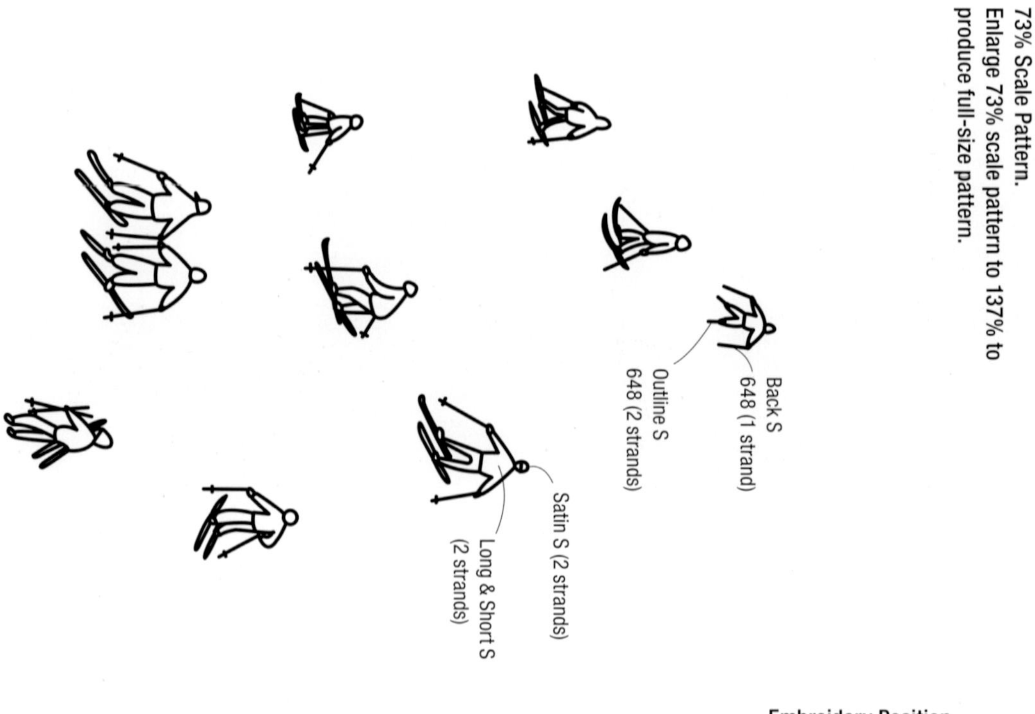

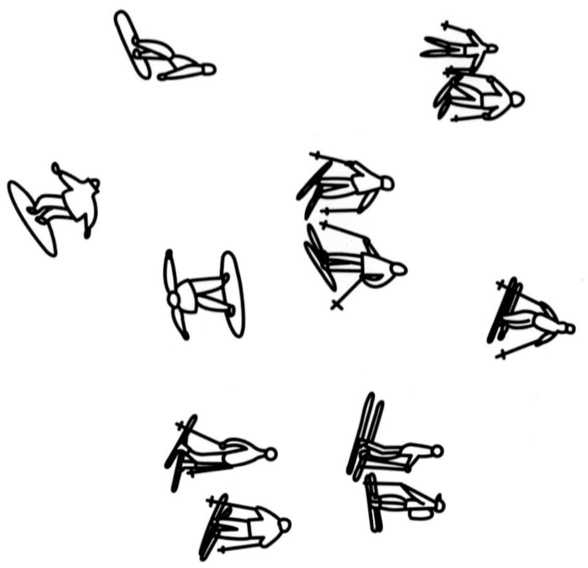

Embroidery Position

Adapt pattern and embroider on any item you desire.

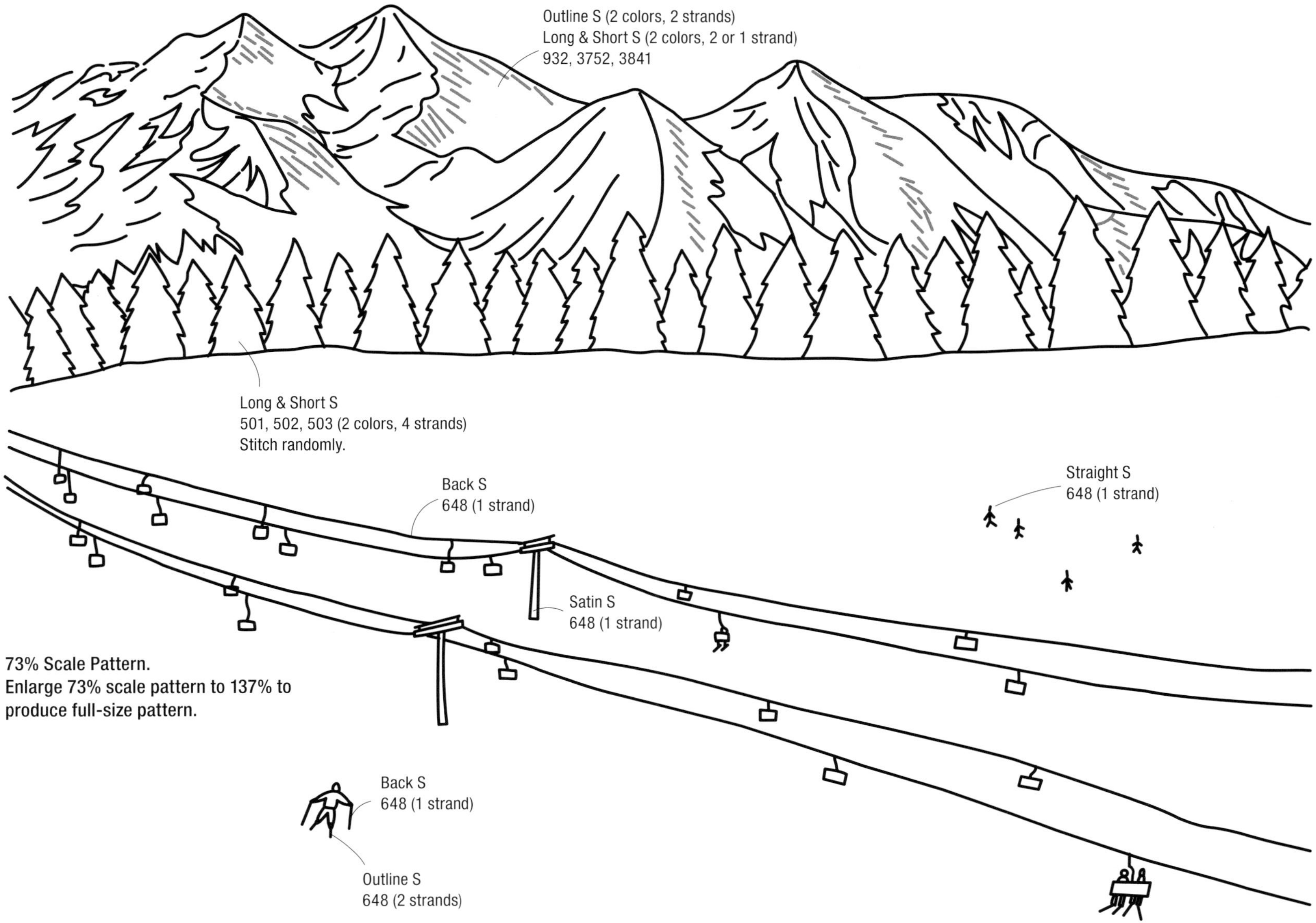

73% Scale Pattern.
Enlarge 73% scale pattern to 137% to produce full-size pattern.

About the Author

Needlework artist Juno embroiders inspiring, beautiful, joyful motifs, and her work is exhibited widely. She lives in Japan.
Instagram: @junoembroidery

Other Schiffer Books on Related Subjects:

Organic Embroidery, Meredith Woolnough, ISBN 978-0-7643-5613-1

The Intentional Thread: A Guide to Drawing, Gesture, and Color in Stitch, Susan Brandeis, ISBN 978-0-7643-5743-5

How to Make Art for Joy's Sake: Free-Spirited Watercolor, Kristy Rice, foreword by Amy Palmer, ISBN 978-0-7643-6151-7

Library of Congress Control Number: 2022944012

ISBN: 978-0-7643-6422-8

Printed in China

Published by Schiffer Publishing, Ltd.
4880 Lower Valley Road
Atglen, PA 19310
Phone: (610) 593-1777; Fax: (610) 593-2002
Email: Info@schifferbooks.com
Web: www.schifferbooks.com

Published in Japanese as *Juno no Shishu Note*

First designed and published in Japan in 2021 by Graphic-sha Publishing Co., Ltd.
English edition published in the United States of America in 2023 by Schiffer Publishing, Ltd.

Original edition creative staff

Photos:	Kiyoko Eto
Book design:	Motoko Kitsukawa
Drawing:	Miyuki Oshima
Editing:	Ayako Enaka (Graphic-sha Publishing)
Cooperation:	GMC, Tsunoda-Shouten

English edition creative staff

English translation:	Kevin Wilson
English edition layout:	Shinichi Ishioka
English edition production and management:	Takako Motoki (Graphic-sha Publishing)